KT-422-170

Hamlet

Hamlet

William Shakespeare

Illustrated by
W. G. Simmonds

LEOPARD

This edition published in Great Britain
in 1995 by Leopard Books,
Random House, 20 Vauxhall Bridge Road,
London SW1V 2SA

Published in the USA
in 1991 by Gramercy Books

Preface and Compilation
Copyright © 1991 by Random House Value Publishing, Inc.
All rights reserved

Grateful acknowledgement is made to
George Weidenfeld & Nicholson Ltd,
for permission to reprint the text used in this edition,
originally published in
The New Temple Shakespeare series,
edited by M. R. Ridley.

Designed by Melissa Ring

ISBN 0 7529 0103 6

Printed and bound in Singapore

8 7 6 5 4 3 2 1

Preface

Hamlet is probably William Shakespeare's most popular and provocative work. The character of Hamlet and the play he inhabits have captivated and intrigued audiences for more than four hundred years. The play is studied in schools, it is endlessly restaged, it has been made into several fine films, and it is constantly quoted. It is embedded in our cultural consciousness.

Shakespeare did not invent the story of Hamlet and his attempt to avenge his father's death. He borrowed the plot and the major characters from a twelfth-century Scandinavian legend. Using this source material, Shakespeare wrote an enormously entertaining example of the popular revenge play, in which he included a ghost, multiple murders, a suicide, madness, incest, adultery, and dazzling swordplay that he knew would please his Elizabethan audience. But Shakespeare also added a completely new dimension to the story, and to the revenge genre, by recasting the character of Hamlet, not as the original legend's single-minded and barbaric avenging angel, but as a complex, rational, and intelligent Renaissance man. It is the very character of Hamlet, perhaps Shakespeare's greatest and most engaging creation, that transforms this play into far more than a blood-and-guts potboiler.

The audience experiences the play through Hamlet's eyes. Hamlet, in his soliloquies, speaks directly to us, and we become the other half of his consciousness. As Hamlet makes his way through the dark, murky, and brutally violent state of Denmark—Shakespeare's microcosm of our world—his questions become our questions, his doubts become our doubts. We share his disillusionment and despair as he ponders the question of mankind's purpose in a world where base corruption and evil appear to be the overwhelming norm of existence. Shakespeare has created in Hamlet an archetypal hero who stands uniquely in our culture's imagination. We identify with Hamlet and see ourselves in him because he represents the ideal image of our humanity—scholar, soldier, and courtier—faced with the puzzling and universal realities of evil and despair.

Shakespeare's plays were first published individually in Quarto editions. Later they were collected and published in Folio editions. There are often variations in the text from edition to edition. The text of this edition of *Hamlet* is the nearest possible approximation to what Shakespeare actually wrote and is based on the earliest reliable printed texts. To avoid distraction, however, the spelling has been modernized. Where a Quarto text exists as well as the First Folio, the passages which occur only in the Quarto are enclosed in square brackets and those which occur only in the Folio are enclosed in brace brackets. The punctuation adheres closely to the Elizabethan punctuation of the early texts and, therefore, is often indicative of the way in which the lines are to be delivered.

This beautiful edition of *Hamlet* is wonderfully illustrated by W. G. Simmonds, the noted English artist, who captures the eerie mood of the play and sets its time and place.

CHRISTOPHER R. MOORE

New York
1991

Dramatis Personæ

CLAUDIUS, *king of Denmark.*
HAMLET, *son to the late, and nephew to the present king.*
POLONIUS, *lord chamberlain.*
HORATIO, *friend to Hamlet.*
LAERTES, *son to Polonius.*
VOLTIMAND,
CORNELIUS,
ROSENCRANTZ, } *courtiers.*
GUILDENSTERN,
OSRIC,
A Gentleman,
A Priest.
MARCELLUS, } *officers.*
BARNARDO,
FRANCISCO, *a soldier.*
REYNALDO, *servant to Polonius.*
Players.
Two clowns, *grave-diggers.*
FORTINBRAS, *prince of Norway.*
A Captain.
English Ambassadors.

GERTRUDE, *queen of Denmark, and mother to Hamlet.*
OPHELIA, *daughter to Polonius.*

Lords, Ladies, Officers, Soldiers, Sailors, Messengers, and other
Attendants.

Ghost of Hamlet's Father.

SCENE: *Denmark.*

Scene I

Elsinore. A platform before the castle
Francisco at his post. Enter to him Barnardo

Barnardo. Who's there?
Francisco. Nay, answer me: stand and unfold yourself.
Barnardo. Long live the king!
Francisco. Barnardo?
Barnardo. He.
Francisco. You come most carefully upon your hour.
Barnardo. 'Tis now struck twelve; get thee to bed, Francisco.
Francisco. For this relief much thanks, 'tis bitter cold,
    And I am sick at heart.
Barnardo. Have you had quiet guard?
Francisco.   Not a mouse stirring.
Barnardo. Well, good night.
    If you do meet Horatio and Marcellus,
    The rivals of my watch, bid them make haste.
Francisco. I think I hear them; Stand ho, who is there?

Enter Horatio and Marcellus

Horatio. Friends to this ground.
Marcellus.   And liegemen to the Dane.
Francisco. Give you good night.
Marcellus.   O, farewell, honest soldier,
    Who hath reliev'd you?
Francisco.   Barnardo hath my place;
    Give you good night.   *Exit*

Marcellus.   Holla, Barnardo!
Barnardo.   Say,
  What, is Horatio there?
Horatio.   A piece of him.
Barnardo. Welcome Horatio, welcome good Marcellus.
Horatio. What, has this thing appear'd again to-night?
Barnardo. I have seen nothing.
Marcellus. Horatio says 'tis but our fantasy,
  And will not let belief take hold of him,
  Touching this dreaded sight twice seen of us;
  Therefore I have entreated him along,
  With us to watch the minutes of this night,
  That if again this apparition come,
  He may approve our eyes and speak to it.
Horatio. Tush, tush, 'twill not appear.
Barnardo.   Sit down a while,
  And let us once again assail your ears,
  That are so fortified against our story,
  What we have two nights seen.
Horatio.   Well, sit we down,
  And let us hear Barnardo speak of this.
Barnardo. Last night of all,
  When yond same star that's westward from the pole
  Had made his course to illume that part of heaven
  Where now it burns, Marcellus and myself,
  The bell then beating one,—

Enter Ghost

Marcellus. Peace, break thee off, look, where it comes again!
Barnardo. In the same figure like the king that's dead.
Marcellus. Thou art a scholar, speak to it, Horatio.
Barnardo. Looks it not like the king? mark it, Horatio.
Horatio. Most like; it horrors me with fear and wonder.
Barnardo. It would be spoke to.
Marcellus.   Speak to it, Horatio.
Horatio. What art thou that usurp'st this time of night,
  Together with that fair and warlike form,
  In which the majesty of buried Denmark

Did sometimes march? by heaven I charge thee speak!
Marcellus. It is offended.
Barnardo.   See, it stalks away.
Horatio. Stay, speak, speak, I charge thee speak!

                                        Exit Ghost

Marcellus. 'Tis gone, and will not answer.
Barnardo. How now, Horatio? you tremble and look pale:
    Is not this something more than fantasy?
    What think you on 't?
Horatio. Before my God I might not this believe,
    Without the sensible and true avouch
    Of mine own eyes.
Marcellus.   Is it not like the king?
Horatio. As thou art to thyself.
    Such was the very armour he had on,
    When he the ambitious Norway combated;
    So frown'd he once, when, in an angry parle,
    He smote the sleaded pollax on the ice.
    'Tis strange.
Marcellus. Thus twice before, and jump at this dead hour,
    With martial stalk hath he gone by our watch.
Horatio. In what particular thought to work I know not,
    But in the gross and scope of my opinion,
    This bodes some strange eruption to our state.
Marcellus. Good now, sit down, and tell me, he that knows,
    Why this same strict and most observant watch
    So nightly toils the subject of the land,
    And why such daily cast of brazen cannon,
    And foreign mart for implements of war,
    Why such impress of shipwrights, whose sore task
    Does not divide the Sunday from the week;
    What might be toward, that this sweaty haste
    Doth make the night joint-labourer with the day:
    Who is 't that can inform me?
Horatio.   That can I.
    At least the whisper goes so; our last king,
    Whose image even but now appear'd to us,
    Was, as you know, by Fortinbras of Norway,

Thereto prick'd on by a most emulate pride,
Dar'd to the combat; in which our valiant Hamlet
(For so this side of our known world esteem'd him)
Did slay this Fortinbras; who by a seal'd compact,
Well ratified by law and heraldry,
Did forfeit, with his life, all those his lands
Which he stood seiz'd of, to the conqueror:
Against the which a moiety competent
Was gaged by our king, which had return'd
To the inheritance of Fortinbras,
Had he been vanquisher; as, by the same cov'nant
And carriage of the article design'd,
His fell to Hamlet; now sir, young Fortinbras,
Of unimproved metal, hot and full,
Hath in the skirts of Norway here and there
Shark'd up a list of lawless resolutes,
For food and diet, to some enterprise
That hath a stomach in 't, which is no other
(As it doth well appear unto our state)
But to recover of us by strong hand
And terms compulsatory, those foresaid lands
So by his father lost; and this, I take it,
Is the main motive of our preparations,
The source of this our watch, and the chief head
Of this post-haste and romage in the land.
[*Barnardo.* I think it be no other, but e'en so;
    Well may it sort that this portentous figure
    Comes armed through our watch so like the king
    That was and is the question of these wars.
Horatio. A mote it is to trouble the mind's eye:
    In the most high and palmy state of Rome,
    A little ere the mightiest Julius fell,
    The graves stood tenantless, and the sheeted dead
    Did squeak and gibber in the Roman streets:

            .   .   .   .   .

    And even the like precurse of fear'd events,
    As harbingers preceding still the fates

And prologue to the omen coming on,
Have heaven and earth together demonstrated
Unto our climatures and countrymen.]
As stars with trains of fire, and dews of blood,
Disasters in the sun; and the moist star,
Upon whose influence Neptune's empire stands,
Was sick almost to doomsday with eclipse:

Re-enter Ghost

But soft, behold, lo where it comes again!
I'll cross it though it blast me; stay, illusion;
If thou hast any sound or use of voice,
Speak to me,
If there be any good thing to be done
That may to thee do ease, and grace to me,
Speak to me,
If thou art privy to thy country's fate,
(Which happily foreknowing may avoid)
O, speak!
Or if thou hast uphoarded in thy life
Extorted treasure in the womb of earth,
For which, they say, your spirits oft walk in death,
Speak of it, stay and speak! (*The cock crows.*) Stop it,
    Marcellus.
Marcellus. Shall I strike it with my partisan?
Horatio. Do, if it will not stand.
Barnardo.   'Tis here!
Horatio.   'Tis here!
Marcellus. 'Tis gone!   *Exit Ghost*
    We do it wrong, being so majestical,
    To offer it the show of violence;
    For it is as the air, invulnerable,
    And our vain blows malicious mockery.
Barnardo. It was about to speak when the cock crew.
Horatio. And then it started like a guilty thing,
    Upon a fearful summons; I have heard,
    The cock that is the trumpet to the morn

Doth with his lofty and shrill-sounding throat
Awake the god of day, and at his warning,
Whether in sea or fire, in earth or air,
The extravagant and erring spirit hies
To his confine; and of the truth herein
This present object made probation.

Marcellus. It faded on the crowing of the cock.
Some say that ever 'gainst that season comes
Wherein our Saviour's birth is celebrated,
The bird of dawning singeth all night long,
And then they say no spirit dare stir abroad,
The nights are wholesome, then no planets strike,
No fairy takes, nor witch hath power to charm,
So hallow'd, and so gracious is that time.

Horatio. So have I heard and do in part believe it.
But look, the morn in russet mantle clad
Walks o'er the dew of yon high eastward hill:
Break we our watch up; and by my advice
Let us impart what we have seen to-night
Unto young Hamlet, for upon my life
This spirit, dumb to us, will speak to him:
Do you consent we shall acquaint him with it,
As needful in our loves, fitting our duty?

Marcellus. Let's do 't, I pray; and I this morning know
Where we shall find him most convenient.   *Exeunt*

Scene II

A room of state in the castle

*Flourish. Enter the King, Queen, Polonius, Laertes,
Voltimand, Cornelius, Lords, Attendants; and Hamlet*

King. Though yet of Hamlet our dear brother's death
The memory be green, and that it us befitted

To bear our hearts in grief, and our whole kingdom
To be contracted in one brow of woe.
Yet so far hath discretion fought with nature
That we with wisest sorrow think on him
Together with remembrance of ourselves:
Therefore our sometime sister, now our queen,
The imperial jointress to this warlike state,
Have we, as 'twere with a defeated joy,
With an auspicious and a dropping eye,
With mirth in funeral, and with dirge in marriage,
In equal scale weighing delight and dole,
Taken to wife: nor have we herein barr'd
Your better wisdoms, which have freely gone
With this affair along. For all, our thanks.
Now follows that you know; young Fortinbras,
Holding a weak supposal of our worth,
Or thinking by our late dear brother's death
Our state to be disjoint, and out of frame,
Colleagued with this dream of his advantage,
He hath not fail'd to pester us with message
Importing the surrender of those lands
Lost by his father, with all bands of law,
To our most valiant brother; so much for him.
Now for ourself, and for this time of meeting,
Thus much the business is; we have here writ
To Norway, uncle of young Fortinbras,
Who, impotent and bed-rid, scarcely hears
Of this his nephew's purpose, to suppress
His further gait herein, in that the levies,
The lists and full proportions, are all made
Out of his subject; and we here dispatch
You good Cornelius, and you Voltimand,
For bearers of this greeting to old Norway,
Giving to you no further personal power
To business with the king, more than the scope
Of these delated articles allow:
Farewell, and let your haste commend your duty.

Cornelius.
Voltimand. } In that and all things will we show our duty.

King. We doubt it nothing, heartily farewell.

Exeunt Voltimand and Cornelius

And now, Laertes, what's the news with you?
You told us of some suit, what is 't, Laertes?
You cannot speak of reason to the Dane
And lose your voice: what wouldst thou beg, Laertes,
That shall not be my offer, not thy asking?
The head is not more native to the heart,
The hand more instrumental to the mouth,
Than is the throne of Denmark to thy father.
What wouldst thou have, Laertes?

Laertes.   My dread lord,
Your leave and favour to return to France,
From whence, though willingly I came to Denmark,
To show my duty in your coronation,
Yet now, I must confess, that duty done,
My thoughts and wishes bend again toward France
And bow them to your gracious leave and pardon.

King. Have you your father's leave? What says Polonius?

Polonius. He hath, my lord, [wrung from me my slow leave
By laboursome petition, and at last
Upon his will I seal'd my hard consent:]
I do beseech you give him leave to go.

King. Take thy fair hour, Laertes; time be thine,
And thy best graces spend it at thy will!
But now, my cousin Hamlet, and my son,—

Hamlet. (*aside*) A little more than kin, and less than kind.

King. How is it that the clouds still hang on you?

Hamlet. Not so [much], my lord; I am too much in the sun.

Queen. Good Hamlet, cast thy nighted colour off,
And let thine eye look like a friend on Denmark;
Do not for ever with thy vailed lids
Seek for thy noble father in the dust;
Thou know'st 'tis common, all that lives must die,
Passing through nature to eternity.

Hamlet. Ay, madam, it is common.

Queen.   If it be,
  Why seems it so particular with thee?

Hamlet. 'Seems,' madam? nay, it is, I know not 'seems.'
  'Tis not alone my inky cloak, good mother,
  Nor customary suits of solemn black,
  Nor windy suspiration of forc'd breath,
  No, nor the fruitful river in the eye,
  Nor the dejected haviour of the visage,
  Together with all forms, moods, shapes of grief,
  That can denote me truly; these indeed seem,
  For they are actions that a man might play,
  But I have that within which passes show,
  These but the trappings and the suits of woe.

King. 'Tis sweet and commendable in your nature, Hamlet,
  To give these mourning duties to your father:
  But you must know your father lost a father,
  That father lost, lost his, and the survivor bound
  In filial obligation for some term
  To do obsequious sorrow; but to persever
  In obstinate condolement is a course
  Of impious stubbornness, 'tis unmanly grief,
  It shows a will most incorrect to heaven,
  A heart unfortified, a mind impatient,
  And understanding simple and unschool'd:
  For what we know must be and is as common
  As any the most vulgar thing to sense,
  Why should we in our peevish opposition
  Take it to heart? Fie! 'tis a fault to heaven,
  A fault against the dead, a fault to nature,
  To reason most absurd, whose common theme
  Is death of fathers, and who still hath cried,
  From the first corse, till he that died to-day,
  'This must be so.' We pray you throw to earth
  This unprevailing woe, and think of us
  As of a father: for let the world take note,
  You are the most immediate to our throne,

And with no less nobility of love
Than that which dearest father bears his son
Do I impart toward you. For your intent
In going back to school in Wittenberg,
It is most retrograde to our desire,
And we beseech you, bend you to remain
Here in the cheer and comfort of our eye,
Our chiefest courtier, cousin, and our son.
Queen. Let not thy mother lose her prayers, Hamlet:
 I pray thee, stay with us; go not to Wittenberg.
Hamlet. I shall in all my best obey you, madam.
King. Why, 'tis a loving and a fair reply:
 Be as ourself in Denmark. Madam, come;
 This gentle and unforc'd accord of Hamlet
 Sits smiling to my heart, in grace whereof,
 No jocund health that Denmark drinks to-day,
 But the great cannon to the clouds shall tell,
 And the king's rouse the heaven shall bruit again,
 Re-speaking earthly thunder. Come away.
                    Flourish. Exeunt all but Hamlet
Hamlet. O that this too too sullied flesh would melt,
 Thaw and resolve itself into a dew,
 Or that the Everlasting had not fix'd
 His canon 'gainst self-slaughter! O God, O God,
 How weary, stale, flat, and unprofitable
 Seem to me all the uses of this world!
 Fie on 't, ah fie! 'tis an unweeded garden
 That grows to seed; things rank and gross in nature
 Possess it merely. That it should come to this!
 But two months dead, nay, not so much, not two;
 So excellent a king, that was to this
 Hyperion to a satyr, so loving to my mother,
 That he might not beteem the winds of heaven
 Visit her face too roughly; heaven and earth,
 Must I remember? why, she should hang on him,
 As if increase of appetite had grown
 By what it fed on, and yet within a month—

Let me not think on 't; frailty, thy name is woman!
A little month, or ere those shoes were old
With which she follow'd my poor father's body,
Like Niobe, all tears:—why she, {even she,—}
O God, a beast that wants discourse of reason
Would have mourn'd longer,—married with my uncle,
My father's brother, but no more like my father
Than I to Hercules: within a month,
Ere yet the salt of most unrighteous tears
Had left the flushing in her galled eyes,
She married; O most wicked speed, to post
With such dexterity to incestuous sheets!
It is not, nor it cannot come to good;
But break my heart, for I must hold my tongue!

Enter Horatio, Marcellus, and Barnardo

Horatio. Hail to your lordship!
Hamlet.   I am glad to see you well:
    Horatio, or I do forget myself.
Horatio. The same, my lord, and your poor servant ever.
Hamlet. Sir, my good friend; I'll change that name with
    you;
    And what make you from Wittenberg, Horatio?
    Marcellus.
Marcellus. My good lord.
Hamlet. I am very glad to see you. (*to Barnardo*) Good
    even, sir.
    (*to Horatio*) But what, in faith, make you from Wit-
    tenberg?
Horatio. A truant disposition, good my lord.
Hamlet. I would not hear your enemy say so,
    Nor shall you do my ear that violence
    To make it truster of your own report
    Against yourself: I know you are no truant:
    But what is your affair in Elsinore?
    We'll teach you for to drink ere you depart.
Horatio. My lord, I came to see your father's funeral.

Hamlet. I prithee, do not mock me, fellow-student;
  I think it was to see my mother's wedding.
Horatio. Indeed, my lord, it follow'd hard upon.
Hamlet. Thrift, thrift, Horatio; the funeral bak'd-meats
  Did coldly furnish forth the marriage tables.
  Would I had met my dearest foe in heaven
  Or ever I had seen that day, Horatio!
  My father, methinks I see my father.
Horatio. Where, my lord?
Hamlet.   In my mind's eye, Horatio.
Horatio. I saw him once; he was a goodly king.
Hamlet. He was a man, take him for all in all,
  I shall not look upon his like again.
Horatio. My lord, I think I saw him yesternight.
Hamlet. Saw? who?
Horatio. My lord, the king your father.
Hamlet.   The king my father?
Horatio. Season your admiration for a while
  With an attent ear, till I may deliver,
  Upon the witness of these gentlemen,
  This marvel to you.
Hamlet.   For God's love, let me hear.
Horatio. Two nights together had these gentlemen,
  Marcellus and Barnardo, on their watch,
  In the dead waste and middle of the night,
  Been thus encounter'd. A figure like your father,
  Armed at point, exactly cap-a-pe,
  Appears before them, and with solemn march
  Goes slow and stately by them: thrice he walk'd
  By their oppress'd and fear-surprised eyes,
  Within his truncheon's length; whilst they distill'd
  Almost to jelly, with the act of fear
  Stand dumb, and speak not to him. This to me
  In dreadful secrecy impart they did,
  And I with them the third night kept the watch:
  Where, as they had deliver'd, both in time,
  Form of the thing, each word made true and good,

The apparition comes: I knew your father,
These hands are not more like.

Hamlet.   But where was this?

Marcellus. My lord, upon the platform where we watch.

Hamlet. Did you not speak to it?

Horatio.   My lord, I did.
But answer made it none; yet once methought
It lifted up it head and did address
Itself to motion, like as it would speak:
But even then the morning cock crew loud,
And at the sound it shrunk in haste away
And vanish'd from our sight.

Hamlet.   'Tis very strange.

Horatio. As I do live my honour'd lord 'tis true,
And we did think it writ down in our duty
To let you know of it.

Hamlet. Indeed, {indeed,} sirs, but this troubles me.
Hold you the watch to-night?

Marcellus. }
Barnardo. }   We do, my lord.

Hamlet. Arm'd, say you?

Marcellus. }
Barnardo. }   Arm'd, my lord.

Hamlet.   From top to toe?

Marcellus. }
Barnardo. } My lord, from head to foot.

Hamlet. Then saw you not his face.

Horatio. O yes, my lord; he wore his beaver up.

Hamlet. What look'd he, frowningly?

Horatio. A countenance more in sorrow than in anger.

Hamlet. Pale, or red?

Horatio. Nay, very pale.

Hamlet.   And fix'd his eyes upon you?

Horatio. Most constantly.

Hamlet.   I would I had been there.

Horatio. It would have much amaz'd you.

Hamlet. Very like, {very like.} Stay'd it long?

Horatio. While one with moderate haste might tell a
   hundred.

Marcellus. ⎫
Barnardo. ⎬ Longer, longer.

Horatio. Not when I saw 't.

Hamlet.   His beard was grizzled, no?

Horatio. It was as I have seen it in his life,
   A sable silver'd.

Hamlet.   I will watch to-night;
   Perchance 'twill walk again.

Horatio.   I warrant it will.

Hamlet. If it assume my noble father's person,
   I'll speak to it, though hell itself should gape
   And bid me hold my peace; I pray you all,
   If you have hitherto conceal'd this sight,
   Let it be tenable in your silence still,
   And whatsoever else shall hap to-night,
   Give it an understanding, but no tongue:
   I will requite your loves; so fare you well:
   Upon the platform, 'twixt eleven and twelve,
   I'll visit you.

All.   Our duty to your honour.

Hamlet. Your loves, as mine to you: farewell.

                         Exeunt all but Hamlet

   My father's spirit——in arms? all is not well;
   I doubt some foul play; would the night were come!
   Till then sit still, my soul: foul deeds will rise,
   Though all the earth o'erwhelm them to men's eyes.   *Exit*

Scene III

Laertes. My necessaries are embark'd: farewell:
    And, sister, as the winds give benefit
    And convoy is assistant, do not sleep,
    But let me hear from you.
Ophelia.   Do you doubt that?
Laertes. For Hamlet, and the trifling of his favour,
    Hold it a fashion, and a toy in blood,
    A violet in the youth of primy nature,
    Forward, not permanent, sweet, not lasting,
    The [perfume and] suppliance of a minute;
    No more.
Ophelia.   No more but so?
Laertes.   Think it no more:
    For nature crescent does not grow alone
    In thews and bulks, but, as this temple waxes,
    The inward service of the mind and soul
    Grows wide withal; perhaps he loves you now,
    And now no soil nor cautel doth besmirch
    The virtue of his will: but you must fear,
    His greatness weigh'd, his will is not his own;
    {For he himself is subject to his birth:}
    He may not, as unvalued persons do,
    Carve for himself, for on his choice depends
    The safety and health of this whole state,
    And therefore must his choice be circumscrib'd
    Unto the voice and yielding of that body
    Whereof he is the head. Then if he says he loves you,
    It fits your wisdom so far to believe it
    As he in his particular act and place
    May give his saying deed, which is no further

Than the main voice of Denmark goes withal.
Then weigh what loss your honour may sustain,
If with too credent ear you list his songs,
Or lose your heart, or your chaste treasure open
To his unmaster'd importunity.
Fear it, Ophelia, fear it, my dear sister,
And keep you in the rear of your affection,
Out of the shot and danger of desire.
The chariest maid is prodigal enough,
If she unmask her beauty to the moon:
Virtue itself 'scapes not calumnious strokes:
The canker galls the infants of the spring
Too oft before their buttons be disclos'd,
And in the morn and liquid dew of youth
Contagious blastments are most imminent.
Be wary then; best safety lies in fear:
Youth to itself rebels, though none else near.
Ophelia. I shall the effect of this good lesson keep
As watchman to my heart; but, good my brother,
Do not as some ungracious pastors do,
Show me the steep and thorny way to heaven,
Whiles a puff'd and reckless libertine,
Himself the primrose path of dalliance treads,
And recks not his own rede.
Laertes.   O, fear me not;
I stay too long: but here my father comes;

Enter Polonius

A double blessing is a double grace,
Occasion smiles upon a second leave.
Polonious. Yet here, Laertes? Aboard, aboard, for shame!
The wind sits in the shoulder of your sail,
And you are stay'd for. There, my blessing with thee,
And these few precepts in thy memory
Look thou character. Give thy thoughts no tongue,
Nor any unproportion'd thought his act;
Be thou familiar, but by no means vulgar;

Those friends thou hast, and their adoption tried,
Grapple them unto thy soul with hoops of steel,
But do not dull thy palm with entertainment
Of each new-hatch'd unfledg'd comrade; beware
Of entrance to a quarrel, but being in,
Bear 't that the opposed may beware of thee;
Give every man thy ear, but few thy voice;
Take each man's censure, but reserve thy judgement;
Costly thy habit as thy purse can buy,
But not express'd in fancy; rich, not gaudy,
For the apparel oft proclaims the man,
And they in France of the best rank and station
Are of a most select and generous chief in that.
Neither a borrower nor a lender be,
For loan oft loses both itself and friend,
And borrowing dulleth edge of husbandry;
This above all, to thine own self be true,
And it must follow, as the night the day,
Thou canst not then be false to any man.
Farewell; my blessing season this in thee!
Laertes. Most humbly do I take my leave, my lord.
Polonius. The time invites you; go, your servants tend.
Laertes. Farewell, Ophelia, and remember well
  What I have said to you.
Ophelia.   'Tis in my memory lock'd,
  And you yourself shall keep the key of it.
Laertes. Farewell.   *Exit*
Polonius. What is 't, Ophelia, he hath said to you?
Ophelia. So please you, something touching the Lord Ham-
  let.
Polonius. Marry, well bethought:
  'Tis told me he hath very oft of late
  Given private time to you, and you yourself
  Have of your audience been most free and bounteous:
  If it be so, as so 'tis put on me,
  And that in way of caution, I must tell you,
  You do not understand yourself so clearly
  As it behoves my daughter, and your honour;
  What is between you? give me up the truth.

Ophelia. He hath, my lord, of late made many tenders
  Of his affection to me.
Polonius. Affection! pooh! you speak like a green girl,
  Unsifted in such perilous circumstance;
  Do you believe his tenders, as you call them?
Ophelia. I do not know, my lord, what I should think.
Polonius. Marry, I will teach you: think yourself a baby,
  That you have ta'en these tenders for true pay,
  Which are not sterling; tender yourself more dearly,
  Or (not to crack the wind of the poor phrase,
  Running it thus) you'll tender me a fool.
Ophelia. My lord, he hath importun'd me with love
  In honourable fashion.
Polonius. Ay, fashion you may call it; go to, go to.
Ophelia. And hath given countenance to his speech, my
    lord,
  With [almost] all the [holy] vows of heaven.
Polonius. Ay, springes to catch woodcocks. I do know,
  When the blood burns, how prodigal the soul
  Lends the tongue vows: these blazes, daughter,
  Giving more light than heat, extinct in both
  Even in their promise, as it is a-making,
  You must not take for fire; from this time
  Be something scanter of your maiden presence,
  Set your entreatments at a higher rate
  Than a command to parley; for Lord Hamlet,
  Believe so much in him, that he is young,
  And with a larger tether may he walk
  Than may be given you: in few, Ophelia,
  Do not believe his vows, for they are brokers,
  Not of that dye which their investments show,
  But mere implorators of unholy suits,
  Breathing like sanctified and pious bawds,
  The better to beguile. This is for all;
  I would not, in plain terms, from this time forth,
  Have you so slander any moment leisure,
  As to give words or talk with the Lord Hamlet.
  Look to 't, I charge you: come your ways.
Ophelia. I shall obey, my lord.   *Exeunt*

Scene IV

Enter Hamlet, Horatio, and Marcellus

Hamlet. The air bites shrewdly; it is very cold.
Horatio. It is a nipping and an eager air.
Hamlet. What hour now?
Horatio.   I think it lacks of twelve.
Marcellus. No, it is struck.
Horatio. Indeed? I heard it not: it then draws near the
     season
   Wherein the spirit held his wont to walk.
                    A flourish of trumpets, and two pieces go off
   What does this mean, my lord?
Hamlet. The king doth wake to-night and takes his rouse,
   Keeps wassail, and the swaggering up-spring reels;
   And as he drains his draughts of Rhenish down,
   The kettle-drum and trumpet thus bray out
   The triumph of his pledge.
Horatio.   Is it a custom?
Hamlet. Ay, marry, is 't,
   But to my mind, though I am native here
   And to the manner born, it is a custom
   More honour'd in the breach than the observance.
   [This heavy-headed revel east and west
   Makes us traduc'd, and tax'd of other nations;
   They clepe us drunkards, and with swinish phrase
   Soil our addition; and indeed it takes
   From our achievements, though perform'd at height,
   The pith and marrow of our attribute.
   So, oft it chances in particular men,
   That for some vicious mole of nature in them,
   As in their birth, wherein they are not guilty,
   (Since nature cannot choose his origin)

By their o'ergrowth of some complexion
Oft breaking down the pales and forts of reason,
Or by some habit, that too much o'er-leavens
The form of plausive manners, that these men,
Carrying, I say, the stamp of one defect,
Being nature's livery, or fortune's star,
His virtues else be they as pure as grace,
As infinite as man may undergo,
Shall in the general censure take corruption
From that particular fault: the dram of eale
Doth all the noble substance of a doubt
To his own scandal.]

Enter Ghost

Horatio.   Look, my lord, it comes!
Hamlet. Angels and ministers of grace defend us!
   Be thou a spirit of health, or goblin damn'd,
   Bring with thee airs from heaven, or blasts from hell,
   Be thy intents wicked, or charitable,
   Thou com'st in such a questionable shape,
   That I will speak to thee, I'll call thee Hamlet,
   King, father, royal Dane: O, answer me,
   Let me not burst in ignorance, but tell
   Why thy canoniz'd bones, hearsed in death,
   Have burst their cerements? why the sepulchre,
   Wherein we saw thee quietly interr'd,
   Hath op'd his ponderous and marble jaws,
   To cast thee up again? What may this mean,
   That thou, dead corse, again in complete steel,
   Revisits thus the glimpses of the moon,
   Making night hideous, and we fools of nature
   So horridly to shake our disposition
   With thoughts beyond the reaches of our souls?
   Say, why is this, wherefore, what should we do?
                                   Ghost beckons

Horatio. It beckons you to go away with it,
As if it some impartment did desire
To you alone.
Marcellus.　　Look with what courteous action
It waves you to a more removed ground:
But do not go with it.
Horatio.　　　　No, by no means.
Hamlet. It will not speak; then I will follow it.
Horatio. Do not, my lord.
Hamlet.　　　　Why, what should be the fear?
I do not set my life at a pin's fee,
And for my soul, what can it do to that,
Being a thing immortal as itself?
It waves me forth again, I'll follow it.
Horatio. What if it tempt you toward the flood, my lord,
Or to the dreadful summit of the cliff
That bettles o'er his base into the sea,
And there assume some other horrible form
What might deprive your sovereignty of reason,
And draw you into madness? think of it:
[The very place puts toys of desperation,
Without more motive, into every brain
That looks so many fathoms to the sea
And hears it roar beneath.]
Hamlet.　　　　It waves me still;
Go on, I'll follow thee.
Marcellus. You shall not go, my lord.
Hamlet.　　　　Hold off your hands.
Horatio. Be rul'd, you shall not go.
Hamlet.　　　　My fate cries out,
And makes each petty arture in this body
As hardy as the Nemean lion's nerve.
Still am I call'd; unhand me gentlemen,
By heaven I'll make a ghost of him that lets me:
I say away, go on, I'll follow thee.
　　　　　　　Exeunt Ghost and Hamlet

Horatio. He waxes desperate with imagination.
Marcellus. Let's follow, 'tis not fit thus to obey him.
Horatio. Have after, to what issue will this come?
Marcellus. Something is rotten in the state of Denmark.
Horatio. Heaven will direct it.
Marcellus.   Nay, let's follow him.

                                        Exeunt

Scene V

Another part of the platform

Enter Ghost and Hamlet

Hamlet. Whither wilt thou lead me? speak; I'll go no
    further.
Ghost. Mark me.
Hamlet.   I will.
Ghost.   My hour is almost come
    When I to sulph'rous and tormenting flames
    Must render up myself.
Hamlet.   Alas, poor ghost!
Ghost. Pity me not, but lend thy serious hearing
    To what I shall unfold.
Hamlet.   Speak; I am bound to hear.
Ghost. So art thou to revenge, when thou shalt hear.
Hamlet. What?
Ghost. I am thy father's spirit,
    Doom'd for a certain term to walk the night,
    And for the day confin'd to fast in fires,
    Till the foul crimes done in my days of nature
    Are burnt and purg'd away: but that I am forbid
    To tell the secrets of my prison-house,
    I could a tale unfold whose lightest word
    Would harrow up thy soul, freeze thy young blood,
    Make thy two eyes like stars start from their spheres,

Thy knotted and combined locks to part,
And each particular hair to stand an end,
Like quills upon the fretful porpentine:
But this eternal blazon must not be
To ears of flesh and blood. List, list, O, list!
If thou didst ever thy dear father love—
Hamlet. O God!
Ghost. Revenge his foul and most unnatural murder.
Hamlet. Murder?
Ghost. Murder most foul, as in the best it is,
But this most foul, strange and unnatural.
Hamlet. Haste me to know 't, that I, with wings as swift
As meditation, or the thoughts of love,
May sweep to my revenge.
Ghost.   I find thee apt,
And duller shouldst thou be than the fat weed
That roots itself in ease on Lethe wharf,
Wouldst thou not stir in this. Now, Hamlet, hear:
'Tis given out, that sleeping in my orchard
A serpent stung me; so the whole ear of Denmark
Is by a forged process of my death
Rankly abus'd: but know, thou noble youth,
The serpent that did sting thy father's life
Now wears his crown.
Hamlet.   O my prophetic soul!
My uncle?
Ghost. Ay, that incestuous, that adulterate beast,
With witchcraft of his wit, with traitorous gifts,—
O wicked wit, and gifts that have the power
So to seduce!—won to his shameful lust
The will of my most seeming-virtuous queen:
O Hamlet, what a falling-off was there
From me, whose love was of that dignity
That it went hand in hand even with the vow
I made to her in marriage, and to decline
Upon a wretch whose natural gifts were poor
To those of mine;

But virtue, as it never will be mov'd,
Though lewdness court it in a shape of heaven,
So lust, though to a radiant angel link'd,
Will sate itself in a celestial bed
And prey on garbage.
But soft! methinks I scent the morning air,
Brief let me be; sleeping within my orchard,
My custom always of the afternoon,
Upon my secure hour thy uncle stole
With juice of cursed hebona in a vial,
And in the porches of my ears did pour
The leperous distilment, whose effect
Holds such an enmity with blood of man,
That swift as quicksilver it courses through
The natural gates and alleys of the body,
And with a sudden vigour it doth possess
And curd, like the eager droppings into milk,
The thin and wholesome blood: so did it mine,
And a most instant tetter bark'd about,
Most lazar-like, with vile and loathsome crust,
All my smooth body.
Thus was I sleeping by a brother's hand
Of life, of crown, of queen, at once dispatch'd,
Cut off even in the blossoms of my sin,
Unhousel'd, disappointed, unannel'd,
No reckoning made, but sent to my account
With all my imperfections on my head:
O, horrible! O, horrible! most horrible!
If thou hast nature in thee, bear it not,
Let not the royal bed of Denmark be
A couch for luxury and damned incest.
But, howsoever thou pursues this act,
Taint not thy mind, nor let thy soul contrive
Against thy mother aught; leave her to heaven,
And to those thorns that in her bosom lodge
To prick and sting her. Fare thee well at once!
The glow-worm shows the matin to be near,

And 'gins to pale his uneffectual fire:
Adieu, adieu, adieu! remember me.   *Exit*
Hamlet. O all you host of heaven! O earth! what else?
 And shall I couple hell? O, fie! Hold, [hold,] my heart,
 And you, my sinews, grow not instant old,
 But bear me stiffly up. Remember thee?
 Ay, thou poor ghost, whiles memory holds a seat
 In this distracted globe. Remember thee?
 Yea, from the table of my memory
 I'll wipe away all trivial fond records,
 All saws of books, all forms, all pressures past
 That youth and observation copied there,
 And thy commandment all alone shall live
 Within the book and volume of my brain,
 Unmix'd with baser matter: yes, by heaven!
 O most pernicious woman!
 O villain, villain, smiling, damned villain,
 My tables, {my tables,}—meet it is I set it down
 That one may smile, and smile, and be a villain,
 At least I am sure it may be so in Denmark.   *Writing*
 So, uncle, there you are; now to my word;
 It is 'Adieu, adieu! remember me.'
 I have sworn 't.
Horatio. (*within*) My lord, my lord!
Marcellus. (*within*)   Lord Hamlet!
Horatio. (*within*)   Heavens secure him!
Hamlet. So be it!
Marcellus. Illo, ho, ho, my lord!
Hamlet. Hillo, ho, ho, boy! come, bird, come.

Enter Horatio and Marcellus

Marcellus. How is 't, my noble lord?
Horatio.   What news, my lord?
Hamlet. O, wonderful!
Horatio. Good my lord, tell it.
Hamlet.   No, you will reveal it.

Horatio. Not I, my lord, by heaven.

Marcellus.   Nor I, my lord.

Hamlet. How say you, then; would heart of man once think
    it?

But you'll be secret?

Horatio. }
Marcellus. }   Ay, by heaven, {my lord.}

Hamlet. There's never a villain dwelling in all Denmark
But he's an arrant knave.

Horatio. There needs no ghost, my lord, come from the
    grave
To tell us this.

Hamlet.   Why, right, you are in the right,
And so, without more circumstance at all,
I hold it fit that we shake hands and part,
You, as your business and desire shall point you,
For every man hath business and desire,
Such as it is, and for my own poor part,
I will go pray.

Horatio. These are but wild and whirling words, my lord.

Hamlet. I am sorry they offend you, heartily;
Yes, faith, heartily.

Horatio.   There's no offence, my lord.

Hamlet. Yes, by Saint Patrick, but there is, Horatio,
And much offence too; touching this vision here,
It is an honest ghost, that let me tell you:
For your desire to know what is between us,
O'ermaster 't as you may; and now, good friends,
As you are friends, scholars, and soldiers,
Give me one poor request.

Horatio. What is 't, my lord? we will.

Hamlet. Never make known what you have seen to-night.

Horatio. }
Marcellus. } My lord, we will not.

Hamlet.   Nay, but swear 't.

Horatio.   In faith,
My lord, not I.

Marcellus.   Nor I, my lord, in faith.

Hamlet. Upon my sword.

Marcellus.   We have sworn, my lord, already.

Hamlet. Indeed, upon my sword, indeed.

>   *Ghost cries under the stage*

Ghost. Swear.

Hamlet. Ha, ha, boy, say'st thou so? art thou there, true-
    penny?
  Come on, you hear this fellow in the cellarage;
  Consent to swear.

Horatio.   Propose the oath, my lord.

Hamlet. Never to speak of this that you have seen,
  Swear by my sword.

Ghost. Swear.

Hamlet. Hic, et ubique? then we'll shift our ground.
  Come hither, gentlemen,
  And lay your hands again upon my sword:
  Swear by my sword,
  Never to speak of this that you have heard.

Ghost. Swear by his sword.

Hamlet. Well said, old mole! canst work i' the earth so fast?
  A worthy pioner! Once more remove, good friends.

Horatio. O day and night, but this is wondrous strange!

Hamlet. And therefore as a stranger give it welcome;
  There are more things in heaven and earth, Horatio,
  Than are dreamt of in your philosophy; but come,
  Here, as before, never, so help you mercy,
  (How strange or odd some'er I bear myself,
  As I perchance hereafter shall think meet
  To put an antic disposition on)
  That you, at such times seeing me, never shall,
  With arms encumber'd thus, or this head-shake,
  Or by pronouncing of some doubtful phrase,
  (As 'Well, well, we know,' or 'We could, an if we would,'
  Or 'If we list to speak,' or 'There be, an if they might,'
  Or such ambiguous giving out) to note
  That you know aught of me: this do swear,
  So grace and mercy at your most need help you.

Ghost. Swear.

Hamlet. Rest, rest, perturbed spirit! (*They swear.*) So,
    gentlemen,
  With all my love I do commend me to you,
  And what so poor a man as Hamlet is
  May do t' express his love and friending to you,
  God willing, shall not lack: let us go in together,
  And still your fingers on your lips, I pray.
  The time is out of joint; O cursed spite,
  That ever I was born to set it right!
  Nay, come, let's go together.   *Exeunt*

Act Two

Scene I

Two months later

A room in Polonius' house

Enter Polonius and Reynaldo

Polonius. Give him this money, and these notes, Reynaldo.
Reynaldo. I will, my lord.
Polonius. You shall do marvellous wisely, good Reynaldo,
    Before you visit him, to make inquire
    Of his behaviour.
Reynaldo.   My lord, I did intend it.
Polonius. Marry, well said, very well said. Look you, sir,
    Inquire me first what Danskers are in Paris,
    And how, and who, what means, and where they keep,
    What company, at what expense, and finding
    By this encompassment and drift of question
    That they do know my son, come you more nearer
    Than your particular demands will touch it:
    Take you, as 'twere, some distant knowledge of him,
    As thus, 'I know his father, and his friends,
    And in part him:' do you mark this, Reynaldo?
Reynaldo. Ay, very well, my lord.
Polonius. 'And in part him; but,' you may say, 'not well:
    But if 't be he I mean, he's very wild,
    Addicted so and so;' and there put on him
    What forgeries you please; marry, none so rank
    As may dishonour him, take heed of that,

But, sir, such wanton, wild, and usual slips
As are companions noted and most known
To youth and liberty.
Reynaldo.   As gaming, my lord.
Polonius. Ay, or drinking, fencing, swearing,
  Quarrelling, drabbing: you may go so far.
Reynaldo. My lord, that would dishonour him.
Polonius. Faith, no, as you may season it in the charge,
  You must not put another scandal on him,
  That he is open to incontinency,
  That's not my meaning, but breathe his faults so quaintly
  That they may seem the taints of liberty,
  The flash and outbreak of a fiery mind,
  A savageness in unreclaimed blood,
  Of general assault.
Reynaldo.   But, my good lord,—
Polonius. Wherefore should you do this?
Reynaldo.   Ay, my lord,
  I would know that.
Polonius.   Marry, sir, here's my drift,
  And I believe it is a fetch of warrant:
  You laying these slight sullies on my son,
  As 'twere a thing a little soil'd with working,
  Mark you,
  Your party in converse, him you would sound,
  Having ever seen in the prenominate crimes
  The youth you breathe of guilty, be assur'd
  He closes with you in this consequence;
  'Good sir,' (or so) or 'friend,' or 'gentleman,'
  According to the phrase or the addition
  Of man and country.
Reynaldo.   Very good, my lord.
Polonius. And then, sir, does he this—he does—what was I
  about to say? By the mass, I was about to say some-
  thing: where did I leave?
Reynaldo. At 'closes in the consequence,' {at 'friend or so,'
  and 'gentleman.'}

Polonius. At 'closes in the consequence,' ay, marry;
He closes {with you} thus: 'I know the gentleman;
I saw him yesterday, or t' other day,
Or then, or then, with such, or such, and, as you say,
There was a' gaming, there o'ertook in 's rouse,
There falling out at tennis:' or perchance,
'I saw him enter such a house of sale,'
Videlicet, a brothel, or so forth. See you now,
Your bait of falsehood takes this carp of truth:
And thus do we of wisdom and of reach,
With windlasses and with assays of bias,
By indirections find directions out:
So, by my former lecture and advice,
Shall you my son. You have me, have you not?
Reynaldo. My lord, I have.
Polonius.   God be wi' ye; fare ye well.
Reynaldo. Good my lord!
Polonius. Observe his inclination in yourself.
Reynaldo. I shall, my lord.
Polonius. And let him ply his music.
Reynaldo.   Well, my lord.
Polonius. Farewell!   *Exit Reynaldo*

Enter Ophelia

                    How now, Ophelia! what's the matter?
Ophelia. O, my lord, my lord, I have been so affrighted!
Polonius. With what, i' the name of God?
Ophelia. My lord, as I was sewing in my closet,
Lord Hamlet, with his doublet all unbrac'd,
No hat upon his head, his stockings foul'd,
Ungarter'd and down-gyved to his ancle,
Pale as his shirt, his knees knocking each other,
And with a look so piteous in purport
As if he had been loosed out of hell
To speak of horrors, he comes before me.
Polonius. Mad for thy love?
Ophelia.   My lord, I do not know,

But truly I do fear it.
Polonius.   What said he?
Ophelia. He took me by the wrist and held me hard;
   Then goes he to the length of all his arm,
   And with his other hand thus o'er his brow,
   He falls to such perusal of my face
   As 'a would draw it. Long stay'd he so;
   At last, a little shaking of mine arm,
   And thrice his head thus waving up and down,
   He rais'd a sigh so piteous and profound
   As it did seem to shatter all his bulk,
   And end his being: that done, he lets me go,
   And with his head over his shoulder turn'd,
   He seem'd to find his way without his eyes,
   For out o' doors he went without their helps,
   And to the last bended their light on me.
Polonius. Come, go with me; I will go seek the king.
   This is the very ecstasy of love,
   Whose violent property fordoes itself
   And leads the will to desperate undertakings
   As oft as any passion under heaven
   That does afflict our natures. I am sorry.
   What, have you given him any hard words of late?
Ophelia. No, my good lord, but, as you did command,
   I did repel his letters, and denied
   His access to me.
Polonius.   That hath made him mad.
   I am sorry that with better heed and judgement
   I had not coted him: I fear'd he did but trifle
   And meant to wreck thee; but beshrew my jealousy!
   By heaven, it is as proper to our age
   To cast beyond ourselves in our opinions
   As it is common for the younger sort
   To lack discretion. Come, go we to the king:
   This must be known, which, being kept close, might move
   More grief to hide than hate to utter love.
   Come.   *Exeunt*

Scene II

A room in the castle

*Flourish. Enter King, Queen, Rosencrantz, Guildenstern,
and Attendants*

King. Welcome, dear Rosencrantz and Guildenstern!
  Moreover that we much did long to see you,
  The need we have to use you did provoke
  Our hasty sending. Something have you heard
  Of Hamlet's transformation; so call it,
  Sith nor the exterior nor the inward man
  Resembles that it was. What it should be,
  More than his father's death, that thus hath put him
  So much from the understanding of himself,
  I cannot dream of: I entreat you both,
  That, being of so young days brought up with him
  And sith so neighbour'd to his youth and haviour,
  That you vouchsafe your rest here in our court
  Some little time, so by your companies
  To draw him on to pleasures, and to gather
  So much as from occasion you may glean,
  Whether aught to us unknown afflicts him thus,
  That open'd lies within our remedy.
Queen. Good gentlemen, he hath much talk'd of you,
  And sure I am two men there is not living
  To whom he more adheres. If it will please you
  To show us so much gentry and good will
  As to expend your time with us a while,
  For the supply and profit of our hope,
  Your visitation shall receive such thanks
  As fits a king's remembrance.
Rosencrantz.   Both your majesties
  Might, by the sovereign power you have of us,
  Put your dread pleasures more into command
  Than to entreaty.

Guildenstern.　　　But we both obey,
　And here give up ourselves, in the full bent,
　To lay our service freely at your feet
　To be commanded.
King. Thanks, Rosencrantz and gentle Guildenstern.
Queen. Thanks, Guildenstern and gentle Rosencrantz:
　And I beseech you instantly to visit
　My too much changed son. Go, some of you,
　And bring these gentlemen where Hamlet is.
Guildenstern. Heavens make our presence and our practices
　Pleasant and helpful to him!
Queen.　　　　　　　　Ay, amen!
　　　　　　　　*Exeunt Rosencrantz, Guildenstern,
　　　　　　　　　　and some Attendants*

　　　　　　　Enter Polonius

Polonius. The ambassadors from Norway, my good lord,
　Are joyfully return'd.
King. Thou still hast been the father of good news.
Polonius. Have I, my lord? Assure you, my good liege,
　I hold my duty as I hold my soul,
　Both to my God, and to my gracious king:
　And I do think, or else this brain of mine
　Hunts not the trail of policy so sure
　As it hath us'd to do, that I have found
　The very cause of Hamlet's lunacy.
King. O, speak of that; that do I long to hear.
Polonius. Give first admittance to the ambassadors;
　My news shall be the fruit to that great feast.
King. Thyself do grace to them, and bring them in.
　　　　　　　　　　　　　Exit Polonius
　He tells me, my dear Gertrude, he hath found
　The head and source of all your son's distemper.
Queen. I doubt it is no other but the main,
　His father's death, and our o'erhasty marriage.
King. Well, we shall sift him.

Re-enter Polonius, with Voltimand and Cornelius

Welcome, my good friends!
Say, Voltimand, what from our brother Norway?
Voltimand. Most fair return of greetings and desires.
Upon our first, he sent out to suppress
His nephew's levies, which to him appear'd
To be a preparation 'gainst the Polack,
But better look'd into, he truly found
It was against your highness; whereat griev'd
That so his sickness, age, and impotence
Was falsely borne in hand, sends out arrests
On Fortinbras, which he in brief obeys,
Receives rebuke from Norway, and in fine
Makes vow before his uncle never more
To give the assay of arms against your majesty.
Whereon old Norway, overcome with joy,
Gives him threescore thousand crowns in annual fee
And his commission to employ those soldiers,
So levied as before, against the Polack,
With an entreaty, herein further shown,   *Giving a paper*
That it might please you to give quiet pass
Through your dominions for this enterprise,
On such regards of safety and allowance
As therein are set down.
King.   It likes us well,
And at our more consider'd time we'll read,
Answer, and think upon this business.
Meantime, we thank you for your well-took labour:
Go to your rest; at night we'll feast together:
Most welcome home!   *Exeunt Voltimand and Cornelius*
Polonius.   This business is well ended.
My liege, and madam, to expostulate
What majesty should be, what duty is,
Why day is day, night night, and time is time,
Were nothing but to waste night, day, and time.
Therefore, for brevity is the soul of wit

And tediousness the limbs and outward flourishes,
I will be brief; your noble son is mad:
Mad call I it, for, to define true madness,
What is 't but to be nothing else but mad?
But let that go.

Queen. More matter, with less art.

Polonius. Madam, I swear I use no art at all.
That he is mad, 'tis true: 'tis true 'tis pity,
And pity 'tis 'tis true: a foolish figure;
But farewell it, for I will use no art.
Mad let us grant him then, and now remains
That we find out the cause of this effect,
Or rather say, the cause of this defect,
For this effect defective comes by cause:
Thus it remains, and the remainder thus.
Perpend;
I have a daughter,—have while she is mine,—
Who in her duty and obedience, mark,
Hath given me this: now gather and surmise.   *Reads*
'To the celestial and my soul's idol, the most beautified
Ophelia,'—
That's an ill phrase, a vile phrase; 'beautified' is a vile
phrase; but you shall hear.   *Reads*
Thus—'in her excellent white bosom, these,' &c.

Queen. Came this from Hamlet to her?

Polonius. Good madam, stay awhile, I will be faithful.

                               Reads

        'Doubt thou the stars are fire,
           Doubt that the sun doth move,
         Doubt truth to be a liar,
           But never doubt I love.

'O dear Ophelia, I am ill at these numbers, I have not art
to reckon my groans, but that I love thee best, O most
best believe it; Adieu.

    'Thine evermore, most dear lady, whilst this machine
        is to him,   HAMLET.'

This in obedience hath my daughter shown me,
And, more above, hath his solicitings,

As they fell out by time, by means, and place,
All given to mine ear.
King.   But how hath she
Receiv'd his love?
Polonius.   What do you think of me?
King. As of a man faithful and honourable.
Polonius. I would fain prove so, but what might you think,
When I had seen this hot love on the wing,
As I perceiv'd it (I must tell you that)
Before my daughter told me, what might you,
Or my dear majesty your queen here, think,
If I had play'd the desk, or table-book,
Or given my heart a winking, mute and dumb,
Or look'd upon this love with idle sight,
What might you think? No, I went round to work,
And my young mistress thus I did bespeak:
'Lord Hamlet is a prince out of thy star;
This must not be:' and then I prescripts gave her,
That she should lock herself from his resort,
Admit no messengers, receive no tokens;
Which done, she took the fruits of my advice;
And he repelled, a short tale to make,
Fell into a sadness, then into a fast,
Thence to a watch, thence into a weakness,
Thence to a lightness, and by this declension
Into the madness wherein now he raves
And all we mourn for.
King. Do you think this?
Queen.   It may be, very like.
Polonius. Hath there been such a time, I 'ld fain know that,
That I have positively said ' 'tis so,'
When it prov'd otherwise?
King.   Not that I know.
Polonius. (*pointing to his head and shoulder*) Take this
from this, if this be otherwise:
If circumstances lead me, I will find
Where truth is hid, though it were hid indeed
Within the centre.
King.   How may we try it further?

Polonius. You know, sometimes he walks four hours to-
gether
Here in the lobby.
Queen.   So he does, indeed.
Polonius. At such a time I'll loose my daughter to him:
Be you and I behind an arras then;
Mark the encounter: if he love her not,
And be not from his reason fall'n thereon,
Let me be no assistant for a state,
But keep a farm and carters.
King.   We will try it.
Queen. But look where sadly the poor wretch comes
reading.
Polonius. Away, I do beseech you, both away:
I'll board him presently; O, give me leave.

Exeunt King, Queen, and Attendants

Enter Hamlet, reading

How does my good Lord Hamlet?
Hamlet. Well, God-a-mercy.
Polonius. Do you know me, my lord?
Hamlet. Excellent {excellent} well, you are a fishmonger.
Polonius. Not I, my lord.
Hamlet. Then I would you were so honest a man.
Polonius. Honest, my lord?
Hamlet. Ay, sir; to be honest, as this world goes, is to be
one man pick'd out of ten thousand.
Polonius. That's very true, my lord.
Hamlet. For if the sun breed maggots in a dead dog, being a
good kissing carrion—Have you a daughter?
Polonius. I have, my lord.
Hamlet. Let her not walk i' the sun: conception is a bless-
ing; but as your daughter may conceive,—friend, look
to 't.
Polonius. (*aside*) How say you by that? Still harping on my
daughter: yet he knew me not at first, 'a said I was a
fishmonger: 'a is far gone {, far gone}: and truly in my
youth I suffer'd much extremity for love; very near this.
I'll speak to him again. What do you read, my lord?

Hamlet. Words, words, words.

Polonius. What is the matter, my lord?

Hamlet. Between who?

Polonius. I mean, the matter that you read, my lord.

Hamlet. Slanders, sir: for the satirical rogue says here that old men have grey beards, that their faces are wrinkled, their eyes purging thick amber and plum-tree gum, and that they have a plentiful lack of wit, together with most weak hams: all which, sir, though I most powerfully and potently believe, yet I hold it not honesty to have it thus set down; for yourself, sir, shall grow old as I am, if like a crab you could go backward.

Polonius. (*aside*) Though this be madness, yet there is method in 't.—Will you walk out of the air, my lord?

Hamlet. Into my grave.

Polonius. Indeed, that's out of the air. (*aside*) How pregnant sometimes his replies are! a happiness that often madness hits on, which reason and sanity could not so prosperously be deliver'd of. I will leave him, {and suddenly contrive the means of meeting between him} and my daughter.—My lord, I will take my leave of you.

Hamlet. You cannot take from me any thing that I will not more willingly part withal: except my life, [except my life, except] my life.

Polonius. Fare you well, my lord.

Hamlet. These tedious old fools!

Re-enter Rosencrantz and Guildenstern

Polonius. You go to seek the Lord Hamlet; there he is.

Rosencrantz. (*to Polonius*) God save you, sir!

Exit Polonius

Guildenstern. My honour'd lord!

Rosencrantz. My most dear lord!

Hamlet. My excellent good friends! How dost thou, Guildenstern? Ah, Rosencrantz! Good lads, how do you both?

Rosencrantz. As the indifferent children of the earth.

Guildenstern. Happy, in that we are not over-happy;
On fortune's cap we are not the very button.

Hamlet. Nor the soles of her shoe?

Rosencrantz. Neither, my lord.

Hamlet. Then you live about her waist, or in the middle of her favours.

Guildenstern. Faith, her privates we.

Hamlet. In the secret parts of Fortune? O, most true; she is a strumpet. What news?

Rosencrantz. None, my lord, but the world's grown honest.

Hamlet. Then is doomsday near: but your news is not true. {Let me question more in particular: what have you, my good friends, deserv'd at the hands of Fortune, that she sends you to prison hither?

Guildenstern. Prison, my lord?

Hamlet. Denmark's a prison.

Rosencrantz. Then is the world one.

Hamlet. A goodly one; in which there are many confines, wards and dungeons; Denmark being one o' the worst.

Rosencrantz. We think not so, my lord.

Hamlet. Why, then 'tis none to you; for there is nothing either good or bad, but thinking makes it so: to me it is a prison.

Rosencrantz. Why then your ambition makes it one; 'tis too narrow for your mind.

Hamlet. O God, I could be bounded in a nut-shell, and count myself a king of infinite space, were it not that I have bad dreams.

Guildenstern. Which dreams indeed are ambition; for the very substance of the ambitious is merely the shadow of a dream.

Hamlet. A dream itself is but a shadow.

Rosencrantz. Truly, and I hold ambition of so airy and light a quality that it is but a shadow's shadow.

Hamlet. Then are our beggars bodies, and our monarchs and outstretch'd heroes the beggars' shadows. Shall we to the court? for, by my fay, I cannot reason.

Rosencrantz. ⎫
Guildenstern. ⎬ We'll wait upon you.

Hamlet. No such matter: I will not sort you with the rest of my servants; for, to speak to you like an honest man, I am most dreadfully attended.} But, in the beaten way of friendship, what make you at Elsinore?

Rosencrantz. To visit you, my lord, no other occasion.

Hamlet. Beggar that I am, I am even poor in thanks; but I thank you: and sure, dear friends, my thanks are too dear a halfpenny. Were you not sent for? is it your own inclining? is it a free visitation? Come, come, deal justly with me: come, come; nay, speak.

Guildenstern. What should we say, my lord?

Hamlet. Any thing but to the purpose. You were sent for, and there is a kind of confession in your looks, which your modesties have not craft enough to colour: I know the good king and queen have sent for you.

Rosencrantz. To what end, my lord?

Hamlet. That you must teach me. But let me conjure you, by the rights of our fellowship, by the consonancy of our youth, by the obligation of our ever-preserv'd love, and by what more dear a better proposer can charge you withal, be even and direct with me, whether you were sent for, or no.

Rosencrantz. (*aside to Guildenstern*) What say you?

Hamlet. (*aside*) Nay then, I have an eye of you.—If you love me, hold not off.

Guildenstern. My lord, we were sent for.

Hamlet. I will tell you why; so shall my anticipation prevent your discovery, and your secrecy to the king and queen moult no feather. I have of late—but wherefore I know not—lost all my mirth, forgone all custom of exercises; and indeed it goes so heavily with my disposition that this goodly frame, the earth, seems to me a sterile promontory, this most excellent canopy, the air, look you, this brave o'erhanging [firmament], this majestical roof fretted with golden fire, why, it appeareth nothing to me but a foul and pestilent congregation of vapours. What piece of work is a man, how noble in reason, how infinite in faculties, in form and moving how express and admirable, in action how like an angel, in apprehension how like a god; the beauty of the world; the paragon of animals; and yet, to me, what is this quintessence of dust? man delights not me, nor women neither, though by your smiling you seem to say so.

Rosencrantz. My lord, there was no such stuff in my thoughts.

Hamlet. Why did ye laugh then, when I said 'man delights not me'?

Rosencrantz. To think, my lord, if you delight not in man, what lenten entertainment the players shall receive from you: we coted them on the way; and hither are they coming, to offer you service.

Hamlet. He that plays the king shall be welcome; his majesty shall have tribute of me; the adventurous knight shall use his foil and target; the lover shall not sigh gratis; the humorous man shall end his part in peace; {the clown shall make those laugh whose lungs are tickle o' the sere,} and the lady shall say her mind freely, or the blank verse shall halt for 't. What players are they?

Rosencrantz. Even those you were wont to take such delight in, the tragedians of the city.

Hamlet. How chances it they travel? their residence, both in reputation and profit, was better both ways.

Rosencrantz. I think their inhibition comes by the means of the late innovation.

Hamlet. Do they hold the same estimation they did when I was in the city? are they so follow'd?

Rosencrantz. No, indeed, are they not.

{*Hamlet.* How comes it? do they grow rusty?

Rosencrantz. Nay, their endeavour keeps in the wonted pace: but there is, sir, an eyrie of children, little eyases, that cry out on the top of question and are most tyrannically clapped for 't: these are now the fashion, and so berattle the common stages—so they call them—that many wearing rapiers are afraid of goose-quills, and dare scarce come thither.

Hamlet. What, are they children? who maintains 'em? how are they escoted? Will they pursue the quality no longer than they can sing? will they not say afterwards, if they should grow themselves to common players,—as it is most

like, if their means are no better,—their writers do them
wrong, to make them exclaim against their own succession?

Rosencrantz. Faith, there has been much to do on both sides,
and the nation holds it no sin to tarre them to contro-
versy: there was for a while no money bid for argument
unless the poet and the player went to cuffs in the
question.

Hamlet. Is 't possible?

Guildenstern. O, there has been much throwing about of
brains.

Hamlet. Do the boys carry it away?

Rosencrantz. Ay, that they do, my lord; Hercules and his
load too.}

Hamlet. It is not very strange, for my uncle is king of Denmark, and those that would make mouths at him while
my father lived, give twenty, forty, fifty, a hundred ducats
a-piece, for his picture in little. 'Sblood, there is something
in this more than natural, if philosophy could find it out.

Flourish of trumpets within

Guildenstern. There are the players.

Hamlet. Gentlemen, you are welcome to Elsinore. Your
hands, come then: the appurtenance of welcome is fashion and ceremony: let me comply with you in this garb,
lest my extent to the players, which, I tell you, must
show fairly outwards, should more appear like entertainment than yours. You are welcome: but my uncle-
father and aunt-mother are deceived.

Guildenstern. In what, my dear lord?

Hamlet. I am but mad north-north-west: when the wind
is southerly I know a hawk from a handsaw.

Re-enter Polonius

Polonius. Well be with you, gentlemen!

Hamlet. Hark you, Guildenstern, and you too, at each ear
a hearer; that great baby you see there is not yet out of
his swaddling clouts.

Rosencrantz. Haply he is the second time come to them,
for they say an old man is twice a child.

Hamlet. I will prophesy; he comes to tell me of the players; mark it. You say right, sir: o' Monday morning; 'twas then indeed.

Polonius. My lord, I have news to tell you.

Hamlet. My lord, I have news to tell you. When Roscius was an actor in Rome,—

Polonius. The actors are come hither, my lord.

Hamlet. Buz, buz!

Polonius. Upon my honour,—

Hamlet. Then came each actor on his ass,—

Polonius. The best actors in the world, either for tragedy, comedy, history, pastoral, pastoral-comical, historical-pastoral, {tragical-historical, tragical-comical-historical-pastoral,} scene individible, or poem unlimited: Seneca cannot be too heavy, nor Plautus too light for the law of writ, and the liberty: these are the only men.

Hamlet. O Jephthah, judge of Israel, what a treasure hadst thou!

Polonius. What a treasure had he, my lord?

Hamlet. Why,
      'One fair daughter, and no more,
        The which he loved passing well.'

Polonius. (*aside*) Still on my daughter.

Hamlet. Am I not i' the right, old Jephthah?

Polonius. If you call me Jephthah, my lord, I have a daughter that I love passing well.

Hamlet. Nay, that follows not.

Polonius. What follows then, my lord?

Hamlet. Why,
        'As by lot, God wot,'
and then you know,
      'It came to pass, as most like it was,'—
the first row of the pious chanson will show you more; for look where my abridgement comes.

Enter the Players

You are welcome, masters, welcome all. I am glad to see thee well. Welcome, good friends. O, old friend! Why, thy face is valanc'd since I saw thee last; com'st thou to

beard me in Denmark? What, my young lady and mistress! By 'r lady, your ladyship is nearer to heaven than
when I saw you last by the altitude of a chopine. Pray
God your voice, like a piece of uncurrent gold, be not
crack'd within the ring. Masters, you are all welcome.
We'll e'en to 't like French falconers, fly at any thing we
see: we'll have a speech straight: come, give us a taste
of your quality: come, a passionate speech.

First Play. What speech, my good lord?

Hamlet. I heard thee speak me a speech once, but it was
never acted, or, if it was, not above once; for the play,
I remember, pleas'd not the million; 'twas caviare to the
general: but it was—as I received it, and others, whose
judgements in such matters cried in the top of mine—
an excellent play, well digested in the scenes, set down
with as much modesty as cunning. I remember, one said
there were no sallets in the lines, to make the matter
savoury, nor no matter in the phrase that might indict the
author of affection; but call'd it an honest method, [as
wholesome as sweet, and by very much more handsome
than fine.] One speech in 't I chiefly lov'd: 'twas Æneas'
talk to Dido, and thereabout of it especially, when he
speaks of Priam's slaughter: if it live in your memory,
begin at this line; let me see, let me see;
'The rugged Pyrrhus, like th' Hyrcanian beast,'—
'Tis not so: it begins with 'Pyrrhus.'
'The rugged Pyrrhus, he whose sable arms,
Black as his purpose, did the night resemble,
When he lay couched in the ominous horse,
Hath now this dread and black complexion smear'd,
With heraldry more dismal head to foot;
Now is he total gules, horridly trick'd
With blood of fathers, mothers, daughters, sons,
Bak'd and impasted with the parching streets
That lend a tyrannous and a damned light
To their lord's murder: roasted in wrath and fire,
And thus o'er-sized with coagulate gore,
With eyes like carbuncles, the hellish Pyrrhus
Old grandsire Priam seeks.'
So, proceed you.

Polonius. 'Fore God, my lord, well spoken, with good accent
and good discretion.

First Play.   'Anon he finds him
Striking too short at Greeks; his antique sword,
Rebellious to his arm, lies where it falls,
Repugnant to command: unequal match'd,
Pyrrhus at Priam drives, in rage strikes wide,
But with the whiff and wind of his fell sword
The unnerved father falls. {Then senseless Ilium,}
Seeming to feel this blow, with flaming top
Stoops to his base; and with a hideous crash
Takes prisoner Pyrrhus' ear, for, lo! his sword,
Which was declining on the milky head
Of reverend Priam, seem'd i the air to stick;
So, as a painted tyrant, Pyrrhus stood,
And like a neutral to his will and matter,
Did nothing.
But as we often see, against some storm,
A silence in the heavens, the rack stand still,
The bold winds speechless, and the orb below
As hush as death, anon the dreadful thunder
Doth rend the region, so after Pyrrhus' pause
A roused vengeance sets him new a-work;
And never did the Cyclops' hammers fall
On Mars's armour, forg'd for proof eterne,
With less remorse than Pyrrhus' bleeding sword
Now falls on Priam.
Out, out, thou strumpet, Fortune! All you gods,
In general synod take away her power,
Break all the spokes and fellies from her wheel,
And bowl the round nave down the hill of heaven
As low as to the fiends!'

Polonius. This is too long.

Hamlet. It shall to the barber's, with your beard.
Prithee, say on: he's for a jig, or a tale of bawdry, or he
sleeps: say on, come to Hecuba.

First Play. 'But who, ah! woe, had seen the mobled
queen—'

Hamlet. 'The mobled queen?'
Polonius. That's good; {'mobled queen' is good.}
First Play. 'Run barefoot up and down, threatening the
  flames
  With bisson rheum, a clout upon that head
  Where late the diadem stood, and for a robe,
  About her lank and all o'er-teemed loins,
  A blanket in the alarm of fear caught up:
  Who this had seen, with tongue in venom steep'd
  'Gainst Fortune's state would treason have pronounc'd;
  But if the gods themselves did see her then,
  When she saw Pyrrhus make malicious sport
  In mincing with his sword her husband's limbs,
  The instant burst of clamour that she made,
  Unless things mortal move them not at all,
  Would have made milch the burning eyes of heaven
  And passion in the gods.'
Polonius. Look, whether he has not turn'd his colour, and
  has tears in 's eyes. Prithee, no more.
Hamlet. 'Tis well; I'll have thee speak out the rest of this
  soon. Good my lord, will you see the players well be-
  stow'd? Do you hear, let them be well us'd, for they
  are the abstract and brief chronicles of the time: after
  your death you were better have a bad epitaph than their
  ill report while you live.
Polonius. My lord, I will use them according to their desert.
Hamlet. God's bodkin, man, much better: use every man
  after his desert, and who shall 'scape whipping? Use them
  after your own honour and dignity; the less they de-
  serve, the more merit is in your bounty. Take them in.
Polonius. Come, sirs.
Hamlet. Follow him, friends: we'll hear a play to-morrow.
  (*exit Polonius with all the Players but the First.*) Dost
  thou hear me, old friend; can you play the Murder of
  Gonzago?
First Play. Ay, my lord.
Hamlet. We'll ha 't to-morrow night. You could, for need,

study a speech of some dozen lines or sixteen lines, which
I would set down and insert in 't, could you not?

First Play. Ay, my lord.

Hamlet. Very well. Follow that lord, and look you mock
him not. [*exit First Player.*] My good friends, I'll leave
you till night: you are welcome to Elsinore.

Rosencrantz. Good my lord!

Hamlet. Ay, so, good bye to you! [*exeunt Rosencrantz and
Guildenstern.*] Now I am alone.

O, what a rogue and peasant slave am I!
Is it not monstrous that this player here,
But in a fiction, in a dream of passion,
Could force his soul so to his own conceit
That from her working all the visage wann'd,
Tears in his eyes, distraction in 's aspect,
A broken voice, and his whole function suiting
With forms to his conceit? and all for nothing,
For Hecuba!
What's Hecuba to him, or he to her,
That he should weep for her? What would he do,
Had he the motive and the cue for passion
That I have? He would drown the stage with tears
And cleave the general ear with horrid speech,
Make mad the guilty, and appal the free,
Confound the ignorant, and amaze indeed
The very faculties of eyes and ears.
Yet I,
A dull and muddy-mettled rascal, peak,
Like John-a-dreams, unpregnant of my cause,
And can say nothing: no, not for a king,
Upon whose property and most dear life
A damn'd defeat was made. Am I a coward,
Who calls me villain, breaks my pate across,
Plucks off my beard, and blows it in my face,
Tweaks me by the nose, gives me the lie i' the throat,
As deep as to the lungs? who does me this?
Ha!
'Swounds, I should take it: for it cannot be
But I am pigeon-liver'd, and lack gall

To make oppression bitter, or ere this
I should ha' fatted all the region kites
With this slave's offal: bloody, bawdy villain,
Remorseless, treacherous, lecherous, kindless villain!
{O, vengeance!}
Why, what an ass am I! This is most brave,
That I, the son of a dear father murder'd,
Prompted to my revenge by heaven and hell,
Must like a whore unpack my heart with words,
And fall a-cursing like a very drab,
A stallion!
Fie upon 't! foh! About, my brains! [Hum,] I have heard
That guilty creatures, sitting at a play,
Have by the very cunning of the scene
Been struck so to the soul, that presently
They have proclaim'd their malefactions;
For murder, though it have no tongue, will speak
With most miraculous organ. I'll have these players
Play something like the murder of my father
Before mine uncle, I'll observe his looks,
I'll tent him to the quick; if 'a do blench,
I know my course. The spirit that I have seen
May be a devil, and the devil hath power
To assume a pleasing shape; yea, and perhaps
Out of my weakness, and my melancholy,
As he is very potent with such spirits,
Abuses me to damn me; I'll have grounds
More relative than this; the play's the thing
Wherein I'll catch the conscience of the king.   *Exit*

Act Three

Scene I

The next day

A room in the castle

*Enter King, Queen, Polonius, Ophelia, Rosencrantz,
and Guildenstern*

King. And can you, by no drift of conference,
    Get from him why he puts on this confusion,
    Grating so harshly all his days of quiet
    With turbulent and dangerous lunacy?
Rosencrantz. He does confess he feels himself distracted,
    But from what cause 'a will by no means speak.
Guildenstern. Nor do we find him forward to be sounded,
    But, with a crafty madness, keeps aloof,
    When we would bring him on to some confession
    Of his true state.
Queen.   Did he receive you well?
Rosencrantz. Most like a gentleman.
Guildenstern. But with much forcing of his disposition.
Rosencrantz. Niggard of question, but of our demands
    Most free in his reply.
Queen.   Did you assay him
    To any pastime?
Rosencrantz. Madam, it so fell out that certain players
    We o'er-raught on the way; of these we told him,
    And there did seem in him a kind of joy
    To hear of it: they are here about the court,
    And, as I think, they have already order
    This night to play before him.
Polonius.   'Tis most true,
    And he beseech'd me to entreat your majesties
    To hear and see the matter.
King. With all my heart; and it doth much content me
    To hear him so inclin'd.

Good gentlemen, give him a further edge,
And drive his purpose into these delights.
Rosencrantz. We shall, my lord.
                    Exeunt Rosencrantz and Guildenstern
King.   Sweet Gertrude, leave us two,
   For we have closely sent for Hamlet hither,
   That he, as 'twere by accident, may here
   Affront Ophelia: her father and myself,
   {Lawful espials,}
   We'll so bestow ourselves that, seeing unseen,
   We may of their encounter frankly judge,
   And gather by him, as he is behav'd,
   If 't be the affliction of his love or no
   That thus he suffers for.
Queen.   I shall obey you.
   And for your part, Ophelia, I do wish
   That your good beauties be the happy cause
   Of Hamlet's wildness; so shall I hope your virtues
   Will bring him to his wonted way again,
   To both your honours.
Ophelia.   Madam, I wish it may.
                                        Exit Queen
Polonius. Ophelia, walk you here. Gracious, so please you,
   We will bestow ourselves. (*to Ophelia*) Read on this
      book,
   That show of such an exercise may colour
   Your loneliness. We are oft to blame in this,—
   'Tis too much prov'd—that with devotion's visage
   And pious action we do sugar o'er
   The devil himself.
King.   (*aside*) O, 'tis too true!
   How smart a lash that speech doth give my conscience!
   The harlot's cheek, beautied with plastering art,
   Is not more ugly to the thing that helps it
   Than is my deed to my most painted word:
   O heavy burthen!
Polonius. I hear him coming: let's withdraw, my lord.
                              Exeunt King and Polonius

Enter Hamlet

Hamlet. To be, or not to be, that is the question;
Whether 'tis nobler in the mind to suffer
The slings and arrows of outrageous fortune,
Or to take arms against a sea of troubles,
And by opposing, end them. To die; to sleep,
No more, and by a sleep to say we end
The heart-ache, and the thousand natural shocks
That flesh is heir to; 'tis a consummation
Devoutly to be wish'd, to die, to sleep;
To sleep; perchance to dream; ay, there's the rub;
For in that sleep of death what dreams may come,
When we have shuffled off this mortal coil,
Must give us pause; there's the respect
That makes calamity of so long life:
For who would bear the whips and scorns of time,
The oppressor's wrong, the proud man's contumely,
The pangs of despis'd love, the law's delay,
The insolence of office, and the spurns
That patient merit of the unworthy takes,
When he himself might his quietus make
With a bare bodkin? who would fardels bear,
To grunt and sweat under a weary life,
But that the dread of something after death,
The undiscover'd country, from whose bourn
No traveller returns, puzzles the will,
And makes us rather bear those ills we have
Than fly to others that we know not of?
Thus conscience does make cowards {of us all,}
And thus the native hue of resolution
Is sicklied o'er with the pale cast of thought,
And enterprises of great pitch and moment
With this regard their currents turn awry
And lose the name of action. Soft you now,
The fair Ophelia! Nymph, in thy orisons
Be all my sins remember'd.
Ophelia.   Good my lord,

How does your honour for this many a day?

Hamlet. I humbly thank you, well, {well, well.}

Ophelia. My lord, I have remembrances of yours,
That I have longed long to re-deliver;
I pray you now receive them.

Hamlet.   No, not I;
I never gave you aught.

Ophelia. My honour'd lord, you know right well you did,
And with them words of so sweet breath compos'd
As made these things more rich: their perfume lost,
Take these again; for to the noble mind
Rich gifts wax poor when givers prove unkind.
There, my lord.

Hamlet. Ha, ha! are you honest?

Ophelia. My lord?

Hamlet. Are you fair?

Ophelia. What means your lordship?

Hamlet. That if you be honest and fair, your honesty
should admit no discourse to your beauty.

Ophelia. Could beauty, my lord, have better converse than
with honesty?

Hamlet. Ay, truly; for the power of beauty will sooner
transform honesty from what it is to a bawd than the
force of honesty can translate beauty into his likeness:
this was sometime a paradox, but now the time gives it
proof. I did love you once.

Ophelia. Indeed, my lord, you made me believe so.

Hamlet. You should not have believ'd me, for virtue cannot
so inoculate our old stock but we shall relish of it: I lov'd
you not.

Ophelia. I was the more deceiv'd.

Hamlet. Get thee to a nunnery; why wouldst thou be a
breeder of sinners? I am myself indifferent honest, but yet
I could accuse me of such things that it were better my
mother had not borne me: I am very proud, revengeful,
ambitious, with more offences at my beck than I have

thoughts to put them in, imagination to give them shape,
or time to act them in. What should such fellows as
I do crawling between earth and heaven? We are arrant knaves, believe none of us, go thy ways to a nunnery.
Where's your father?

Ophelia. At home, my lord.

Hamlet. Let the doors be shut upon him, that he may play
the fool no where but in 's own house. Farewell.

Ophelia. O, help him, you sweet heavens!

Hamlet. If thou dost marry, I'll give thee this plague for
thy dowry: be thou as chaste as ice, as pure as snow,
thou shalt not escape calumny. Get thee to a nunnery,
farewell. Or, if thou wilt needs marry, marry a fool, for
wise men know well enough what monsters you make of
them. To a nunnery, go, and quickly too, farewell.

Ophelia. Heavenly powers restore him!

Hamlet. I have heard of your paintings well enough; God
hath given you one face, and you make yourselves
another: you jig and amble; an you list you nick-
name God's creatures, and make your wantonness
ignorance. Go to, I'll no more on 't, it hath made
me mad. I say we will have no more marriage; those that
are married already, all but one shall live, the rest shall
keep as they are. To a nunnery, go.   *Exit*

Ophelia. O, what a noble mind is here o'erthrown!
The courtier's, soldier's, scholar's, eye, tongue, sword,
The expectancy and rose of the fair state,
The glass of fashion, and the mould of form,
The observ'd of all observers, quite, quite down,
And I of ladies most deject and wretched,
That suck'd the honey of his music'd vows;
Now see that noble and most sovereign reason,
Like sweet bells jangled out of time, and harsh,
That unmatch'd form, and stature of blown youth,
Blasted with ecstasy: O, woe is me,
To have seen what I have seen, see what I see!

Re-enter King and Polonius

King. Love! his affections do not that way tend,
  Nor what he spake, though it lack'd form a little,
  Was not like madness. There's something in his soul
  O'er which his melancholy sits on brood,
  And I do doubt the hatch and the disclose
  Will be some danger: which [for] to prevent,
  I have in quick determination
  Thus set it down:—he shall with speed to England,
  For the demand of our neglected tribute:
  Haply the seas, and countries different,
  With variable objects, shall expel
  This something-settled matter in his heart,
  Whereon his brains still beating puts him thus
  From fashion of himself. What think you on 't?
Polonius. It shall do well: but yet do I believe
  The origin and commencement of his grief
  Sprung from neglected love. How now, Ophelia?
  You need not tell us what Lord Hamlet said,
  We heard it all. My lord, do as you please;
  But if you hold it fit, after the play,
  Let his queen mother all alone entreat him
  To show his grief; let her be round with him;
  And I'll be plac'd, so please you, in the ear
  Of all their conference. If she find him not,
  To England send him; or confine him where
  Your wisdom best shall think.
King.   It shall be so:
  Madness in great ones must not unwatch'd go.   *Exeunt*

Scene II

Enter Hamlet and three of the Players

Hamlet. Speak the speech, I pray you, as I pronounc'd it
to you, trippingly on the tongue; but if you mouth it as
many of our players do, I had as lief the towncrier spoke
my lines; nor do not saw the air too much with your
hand thus, but use all gently, for in the very torrent, tem-
pest, and, as I may say, whirlwind of your passion, you
must acquire and beget a temperance, that may give it
smoothness. O, it offends me to the soul to hear a robusti-
ous periwig-pated fellow tear a passion to tatters, to very
rags, to split the ears of the groundlings, who for the
most part are capable of nothing but inexplicable dumb-
shows, and noise: I would have such a fellow whipp'd for
o'erdoing Termagant; it out-herods Herod: pray you,
avoid it.

First Play. I warrant your honour.

Hamlet. Be not too tame neither, but let your own discretion be your tutor, suit the action to the word, the word
to the action, with this special observance, that you o'er-
step not the modesty of nature: for anything so o'erdone
is from the purpose of playing, whose end, both at the
first, and now, was and is, to hold as 'twere the mirror up
to nature, to show virtue her {own} feature, scorn her own
image, and the very age and body of the time his form
and pressure. Now this overdone, or come tardy off,
though it makes the unskilful laugh, cannot but make the
judicious grieve, the censure of which one must in your
allowance o'erweigh a whole theatre of others. O, there
be players that I have seen play, and heard others praise,
and that highly, not to speak it profanely, that neither
having the accent of Christians, nor the gait of Christian,

pagan, nor man, have so strutted and bellow'd, that I have thought some of nature's journeymen had made men, and not made them well, they imitated humanity so abhominably.

First Play. I hope we have reform'd that indifferently with us.

Hamlet. O, reform it altogether; and let those that play your clowns speak no more than is set down for them: for there be of them that will themselves laugh, to set on some quantity of barren spectators to laugh too, though in thee mean time some necessary question of the play be then to be consider'd: that's villainous, and shows a most pitiful ambition in the fool that uses it. Go, make you ready.

Exeunt Players

Enter Polonius, Rosencrantz, and Guildenstern

How now, my lord? will the king hear this piece of work?

Polonius. And the queen too, and that presently.

Hamlet. Bid the players make haste.   *Exit Polonius*
Will you two help to hasten them?

Rosencrantz. ⎱
Guildenstern. ⎰ Ay, my lord.

Exeunt Rosencrantz and Guildenstern

Hamlet. What ho! Horatio!

Enter Horatio

Horatio. Here, sweet lord, at your service.

Hamlet. Horatio, thou art e'en as just a man
  As e'er my conversation cop'd withal.

Horatio. O, my dear lord,—

Hamlet.   Nay, do not think I flatter,
  For what advancement may I hope from thee,
  That no revenue hast but thy good spirits,
  To feed and clothe thee? Why should the poor be flatter'd?.
  No, let the candied tongue lick absurd pomp,
  And crook the pregnant hinges of the knee

Where thrift may follow fawning. Dost thou hear?
Since my dear soul was mistress of her choice,
And could of men distinguish her election,
S'hath seal'd thee for herself, for thou hast been
As one, in suffering all, that suffers nothing,
A man that fortune's buffets and rewards
Hast ta'en with equal thanks: and blest are those
Whose blood and judgement are so well commedled
That they are not a pipe for fortune's finger
To sound what stop she please. Give me that man
That is not passion's slave, and I will wear him
In my heart's core, ay, in my heart of heart,
As I do thee. Something too much of this.
There is a play to-night before the king;
One scene of it comes near the circumstance
Which I have told thee of my father's death:
I prithee, when thou seest that act a-foot,
Even with the very comment of thy soul
Observe my uncle; if his occulted guilt
Do not itself unkennel in one speech,
It is a damned ghost that we have seen,
And my imaginations are as foul
As Vulcan's stithy. Give him heedful note;
For I mine eyes will rivet to his face,
And after we will both our judgements join
In censure of his seeming.
Horatio.   Well, my lord:
If 'a steal aught the whilst this play is playing,
And 'scape detecting, I will pay the theft.
Hamlet. They are coming to the play: I must be idle:
Get you a place.

Danish march. A flourish. Enter King, Queen, Polonius, Ophelia, Rosencrantz, Guildenstern, and other Lords attendant, with the Guard carrying torches

King. How fares our cousin Hamlet?
Hamlet. Excellent, i' faith, of the chameleon's dish: I eat
the air, promise-cramm'd: you cannot feed capons so.

King. I have nothing with this answer, Hamlet; these words
are not mine.

Hamlet. No, nor mine now. [*to Polonius*] My lord, you
play'd once i' the university, you say?

Polonius. That did I, my lord, and was accounted a good
actor.

Hamlet. What did you enact?

Polonius. I did enact Julius Cæsar, I was killed i' the
Capitol, Brutus kill'd me.

Hamlet. It was a brute part of him to kill so capital a calf
there. Be the players ready?

Rosencrantz. Ay, my lord, they stay upon your patience.

Queen. Come hither, my dear Hamlet, sit by me.

Hamlet. No, good mother, here's metal more attractive.

Polonius. (*to the King*) O, ho! do you mark that?

Hamlet. Lady, shall I lie in your lap?
                              Lying down at Ophelia's feet

Ophelia. No, my lord.

{*Hamlet.* I mean, my head upon your lap?

Ophelia. Ay, my lord.}

Hamlet. Do you think I meant country matters?

Ophelia. I think nothing, my lord.

Hamlet. That's a fair thought to lie between maids' legs.

Ophelia. What is, my lord?

Hamlet. Nothing.

Ophelia. You are merry, my lord.

Hamlet. Who, I?

Ophelia. Ay, my lord.

Hamlet. O God, your only jig-maker. What should a man
do but be merry? for look you how cheerfully my mother
looks, and my father died within 's two hours.

Ophelia. Nay, 'tis twice two months, my lord.

Hamlet. So long? Nay then, let the devil wear black, for I'll
have a suit of sables. O heavens! die two months ago,
and not forgotten yet? Then there's hope a great man's
memory may outlive his life half a year: but, by 'r lady,
'a must build churches then, or else shall 'a suffer not

thinking on, with the hobby-horse, whose epitaph is, 'For,
O, for, O, the hobby-horse is forgot.'

The trumpets sound. The dumb-show enters

*Enter a King and a Queen, the Queen embracing him, and he
her. He takes her up, and declines his head upon her neck: he
lies him down upon a bank of flowers: she, seeing him asleep,
leaves him. Anon come in another man, takes off his crown, kisses
it, pours poison in the sleeper's ears, and leaves him. The Queen
returns, finds the King dead, makes passionate action. The
Poisoner with some three or four come in again, seem to con-
dole with her. The dead body is carried away. The Poisoner
woos the Queen with gifts: she seems harsh awhile, but in the
end accepts love*   *Exeunt*

Ophelia. What means this, my lord?
Hamlet. Marry, this is miching mallecho; it means mischief.
Ophelia. Belike this show imports the argument of the play.

Enter Prologue

Hamlet. We shall know by this fellow: the players cannot
    keep {counsel}; they'll tell all.
Ophelia. Will 'a tell us what this show meant?
Hamlet. Ay, or any show that you will show him: be not
    you asham'd to show, he'll not shame to tell you what it
    means.
Ophelia. You are naught, you are naught: I'll mark the play.
Prologue.   For us and for our tragedy,
                 Here stooping to your clemency,
                 We beg your hearing patiently.
Hamlet. Is this a prologue, or the posy of a ring?
Ophelia. 'Tis brief, my lord.
Hamlet. As woman's love.

Enter two Players, King and Queen

Play. King. Full thirty times hath Phœbus' cart gone round
    Neptune's salt wash and Tellus' orbed ground,
    And thirty dozen moons with borrow'd sheen
    About the world have times twelve thirties been,

Since love our hearts, and Hymen did our hands,
Unite commutual in most sacred bands.
Play. Queen. So many journeys may the sun and moon
Make us again count o'er ere love be done!
But, woe is me, you are so sick of late,
So far from cheer and from our former state,
That I distrust you. Yet, though I distrust,
Discomfort you, my lord, it nothing must:
For [women fear too much, even as they love,
And] women's fear and love hold quantity,
[Either none,] in neither ought, or in extremity;
Now, what my love is, proof hath made you know,
And as my love is siz'd, my fear is so:
[Where love is great, the littlest doubts are fear,
Where little fears grow great, great love grows there.]
Play. King. Faith, I must leave thee, love, and shortly too;
My operant powers their functions leave to do:
And thou shalt live in this fair world behind,
Honour'd, belov'd; and haply one as kind
For husband shalt thou—
Play. Queen.　　　　　O, confound the rest
Such love must needs be treason in my breast:
In second husband let me be accurst,
None wed the second but who kill'd the first.
Hamlet. (aside) That's wormwood.
Play. Queen. The instances that second marriage move
Are base respects of thrift, but none of love:
A second time I kill my husband dead,
When second husband kisses me in bed.
Play. King. I do believe you think what now you speak,
But what we do determine, oft we break.
Purpose is but the slave to memory,
Of violent birth, but poor validity:
Which now, the fruit unripe, sticks on the tree,
But fall unshaken when they mellow be.
Most necessary 'tis that we forget
To pay ourselves what to ourselves is debt:
What to ourselves in passion we propose,

The passion ending, doth the purpose lose.
The violence of either, grief or joy,
Their own enactures with themselves destroy:
Where joy most revels, grief doth most lament;
Grief joys, joy grieves, on slender accident.
This world is not for aye, nor 'tis not strange
That even our loves should with our fortunes change:
For 'tis a question left us yet to prove,
Whether love lead fortune, or else fortune love.
The great man down, you mark his favourite flies;
The poor advanc'd makes friends of enemies:
And hitherto doth love on fortune tend:
For who not needs shall never lack a friend,
And who in want a hollow friend doth try
Directly seasons him his enemy.
But, orderly to end where I begun,
Our wills and fates do so contrary run,
That our devices still are overthrown,
Our thoughts are ours, their ends none of our own:
So think thou wilt no second husband wed,
But die thy thoughts when thy first lord is dead.

Play. Queen. Nor earth to me give food, nor heaven light!
Sport and repose lock from me day and night!
[To desperation turn my trust and hope,
And anchor's cheer in prison be my scope!]
Each opposite, that blanks the face of joy,
Meet what I would have well and it destroy!
Both here and hence pursue me lasting strife,
If, once a widow, ever I be a wife!

Hamlet. If she should break it now!

Play. King. 'Tis deeply sworn. Sweet, leave me here a while;
My spirits grow dull, and fain I would beguile
The tedious day with sleep.   *Sleeps*

Play. Queen.　　　　　　　Sleep rock thy brain,
And never come mischance between us twain!　　*Exit*
Hamlet. Madam, how like you this play?

Queen. The lady doth protest too much, methinks.

Hamlet. O, but she'll keep her word.

King. Have you heard the argument? Is there no offence
in 't?

Hamlet. No, no, they do but jest, poison in jest; no offence
i' the world.

King. What do you call the play?

Hamlet. The Mouse-trap. Marry, how? Tropically. This play
is the image of a murder done in Vienna: Gonzago is
the duke's name, his wife, Baptista: you shall see anon,
'tis a knavish piece of work, but what of that? your majesty, and we that have free souls, it touches us not: let
the gall'd jade wince, our withers are unwrung.

Enter Lucianus

This is one Lucianus, nephew to the king.

Ophelia. You are as good as a chorus, my lord.

Hamlet. I could interpret between you and your love, if I
could see the puppets dallying.

Ophelia. You are keen, my lord, you are keen.

Hamlet. It would cost you a groaning to take off mine edge.

Ophelia. Still better and worse.

Hamlet. So you mis-take your husbands. Begin, murderer,
{pox,} leave thy damnable faces, and begin; come, the
croaking raven doth bellow for revenge.

Lucianus. Thoughts black, hands apt, drugs fit, and time
agreeing;
Confederate season, else no creature seeing;
Thou mixture rank, of midnight weeds collected,
With Hecat's ban thrice blasted, thrice infected,

Thy natural magic, and dire property,
On wholesome life usurps immediately.
                    Pours the poison into the sleeper's ear
Hamlet. He poisons him i' the garden for his estate, his
    name's Gonzago, the story is extant, and written in very
    choice Italian, you shall see anon how the murderer gets
    the love of Gonzago's wife.
Ophelia. The king rises.
{*Hamlet.* What, frighted with false fire?}
Queen. How fares my lord?
Polonius. Give o'er the play.
King. Give me some light. Away!
Polonius. Lights, lights, lights.
                    Exeunt all but Hamlet and Horatio
Hamlet.   Why, let the stricken deer go weep,
            The hart ungalled play;
        For some must watch, while some must sleep:
            Thus runs the world away.
Would not this, sir, and a forest of feathers—if the rest
    of my fortunes turn Turk with me—with Provincial roses
    on my raz'd shoes, get me a fellowship in a cry of players?
Horatio. Half a share.
Hamlet. A whole one, I.
            For thou dost know, O Damon dear,
                This realm dismantled was
            Of Jove himself; and now reigns here
                A very, very—pacock.
Horatio. You might have rhym'd.
Hamlet. O good Horatio, I'll take the ghost's word for a
    thousand pound. Didst perceive?
Horatio. Very well, my lord.
Hamlet. Upon the talk of the poisoning?
Horatio. I did very well note him.
Hamlet. Ah, ha! Come, some music! come, the recorders!
            For if the king like not the comedy,
            Why then, belike, he likes it not, perdy.
Come, some music!

Re-enter Rosencrantz and Guildenstern

Guildenstern. Good my lord, vouchsafe me a word with
you.

Hamlet. Sir, a whole history.

Guildenstern. The king, sir,—

Hamlet. Ay, sir, what of him?

Guildenstern. Is in his retirement marvellous distemper'd.

Hamlet. With drink, sir?

Guildenstern. No, my lord, with choler.

Hamlet. Your wisdom should show itself more richer to
signify this to the doctor; for, for me to put him to his
purgation would perhaps plunge him into more choler.

Guildenstern. Good my lord, put your discourse into some
frame, and start not so wildly from my affair.

Hamlet. I am tame, sir; pronounce.

Guildenstern. The queen, your mother, in most great affliction of spirit, hath sent me to you.

Hamlet. You are welcome.

Guildenstern. Nay, good my lord, this courtesy is not of the
right breed. If it shall please you to make me a wholesome answer, I will do your mother's commandment:
if not, your pardon and my return shall be the end of
business.

Hamlet. Sir, I cannot.

Guildenstern. What, my lord?

Hamlet. Make you a wholesome answer; my wit's diseas'd:
but, sir, such answer as I can make, you shall command,
or rather, as you say, my mother: therefore no more, but
to the matter; my mother, you say,—

Rosencrantz. Then thus she says; your behaviour hath
struck her into amazement and admiration.

Hamlet. O wonderful son, that can so stonish a mother!
But is there no sequel at the heels of this mother's admiration? Impart.

Rosencrantz. She desires to speak with you in her closet
ere you go to bed.

Hamlet. We shall obey, were she ten times our mother. Have you any further trade with us?

Rosencrantz. My lord, you once did love me.

Hamlet. And do still, by these pickers and stealers.

Rosencrantz. Good my lord, what is your cause of distemper? You do surely bar the door upon your own liberty, if you deny your griefs to your friend.

Hamlet. Sir, I lack advancement.

Rosencrantz. How can that be, when you have the voice of the king himself for your succession in Denmark?

Hamlet. Ay, sir, but 'while the grass grows,'—the proverb is something musty.

Re-enter Players with recorders

O, the recorders! let me see one. To withdraw with you: —why do you go about to recover the wind of me, as if you would drive me into a toil?

Guildenstern. O, my lord, if my duty be too bold, my love is too unmannerly.

Hamlet. I do not well understand that. Will you play upon this pipe?

Guildenstern. My lord, I cannot.

Hamlet. I pray you.

Guildenstern. Believe me, I cannot.

Hamlet. I do beseech you.

Guildenstern. I know no touch of it, my lord.

Hamlet. It is as easy as lying: govern these ventages with your fingers and thumbs, give it breath with your mouth, and it will discourse most eloquent music; look you, these are the stops.

Guildenstern. But these cannot I command to any utterance of harmony; I have not the skill.

Hamlet. Why, look you now how unworthy a thing you make of me! You would play upon me, you would seem to know my stops, you would pluck out the heart of my mystery, you would sound me from my lowest note

to {the top of} my compass; and there is much music,
excellent voice, in this little organ, yet cannot you make
it speak. 'Sblood, do you think I am easier to be play'd
on than a pipe? Call me what instrument you will, though
you can fret me, yet you cannot play upon me.

Re-enter Polonius

God bless you, sir!
Polonius. My lord, the queen would speak with you, and
presently.
Hamlet. Do you see yonder cloud that's almost in shape
of a camel?
Polonius. By the mass and 'tis, like a camel indeed.
Hamlet. Methinks it is like a weasel.
Polonius. It is back'd like a weasel.
Hamlet. Or like a whale.
Polonius. Very like a whale.
Hamlet. Then I will come to my mother by and by. (*aside*)
They fool me to the top of my bent. I will come by and
by. Leave me, friends. I will, say so.
                                         Exeunt all but Hamlet

'By and by' is easily said.
'Tis now the very witching time of night,
When churchyards yawn, and hell itself breaks out
Contagion to this world: now could I drink hot blood,
And do such bitter business as the day
Would quake to look on. Soft! now to my mother.
O heart, lose not thy nature, let not ever
The soul of Nero enter this firm bosom;
Let me be cruel, not unnatural:
I will speak daggers to her, but use none;
My tongue and soul in this be hypocrites;
How in my words somever she be shent,
To give them seals never my soul consent!   *Exit*

Scene III

Enter King, Rosencrantz, and Guildenstern

King. I like him not, nor stands it safe with us
  To let his madness range. Therefore prepare you;
  I your commission will forthwith dispatch,
  And he to England shall along with you:
  The terms of our estate may not endure
  Hazard so near us as doth hourly grow
  Out of his braves.
Guildenstern.   We will ourselves provide:
  Most holy and religious fear it is
  To keep those many many bodies safe
  That live and feed upon your majesty.
Rosencrantz. The single and peculiar life is bound
  With all the strength and armour of the mind
  To keep itself from noyance, but much more
  That spirit upon whose weal depends and rests
  The lives of many. The cease of majesty
  Dies not alone, but like a gulf doth draw
  What's near it with it: or it is a massy wheel,
  Fix'd on the summit of the highest mount,
  To whose huge spokes ten thousand lesser things
  Are mortis'd and adjoin'd, which when it falls,
  Each small annexment, petty consequence,
  Attends the boisterous ruin. Never alone
  Did the king sigh, but with a general groan.
King. Arm you, I pray you, to this speedy voyage,

For we will fetters put about this fear,
Which now goes too free-footed.

Rosencrantz. ⎱
Guildenstern. ⎰   We will haste us.

       Exeunt Rosencrantz and Guildenstern

       Enter Polonius

Polonius. My lord, he's going to his mother's closet:
  Behind the arras I'll convey myself,
  To hear the process: I'll warrant she'll tax him home:
  And, as you said, and wisely was it said,
  'Tis meet that some more audience than a mother,
  Since nature makes them partial, should o'erhear
  The speech of vantage. Fare you well, my liege;
  I'll call upon you ere you go to bed,
  And tell you what I know.

King.   Thanks, dear my lord.

                   Exit Polonius

O, my offence is rank, it smells to heaven,
It hath the primal eldest curse upon 't,
A brother's murder. Pray can I not;
Though inclination be as sharp as will,
My stronger guilt defeats my strong intent,
And like a man to double business bound,
I stand in pause where I shall first begin,
And both neglect. What if this cursed hand
Were thicker than itself with brother's blood,
Is there not rain enough in the sweet heavens
To wash it white as snow? Whereto serves mercy
But to confront the visage of offence?
And what's in prayer but this twofold force,
To be forestalled ere we come to fall,
Or pardon'd being down? Then I'll look up;
My fault is past. But O, what form of prayer
Can serve my turn? 'Forgive me my foul murder?'
That cannot be, since I am still possess'd

Of those effects for which I did the murder,
My crown, mine own ambition and my queen.
May one be pardon'd and retain the offence?
In the corrupted currents of this world
Offence's gilded hand may shove by justice,
And oft 'tis seen the wicked prize itself
Buys out the law: but 'tis not so above;
There is no shuffling, there the action lies
In his true nature, and we ourselves compell'd
Even to the teeth and forehead of our faults
To give in evidence. What then? what rests?
Try what repentance can: what can it not?
Yet what can it when one can not repent?
O wretched state! O bosom black as death!
O limed soul, that struggling to be free
Art more engag'd! Help, angels! make assay!
Bow, stubborn knees, and, heart with strings of steel,
Be soft as sinews of the new-born babe!
All may be well.   *Retires and kneels*

Enter Hamlet

Hamlet. Now might I do it, but now 'a is a-praying;
And now I'll do it, and so he goes to heaven,
And so am I reveng'd? That would be scann'd;
A villain kills my father, and for that,
I, his sole son, do this same villain send
To heaven.
Why, this is hire and salary, not revenge.
'A took my father grossly, full of bread.
With all his crimes broad blown, as flush as May;
And how his audit stands who knows save heaven?
But in our circumstance and course of thought,
'Tis heavy with him: and am I then reveng'd,
To take him in the purging of his soul,
When he is fit and season'd for his passage?
No.

Up, sword, and know thou a more horrid hent,
When he is drunk, asleep, or in his rage,
Or in the incestuous pleasure of his bed,
At game, a-swearing, or about some act
That has no relish of salvation in 't,
Then trip him, that his heels may kick at heaven,
And that his soul may be as damn'd and black
As hell whereto it goes. My mother stays:
This physic but prolongs thy sickly days.   *Exit*
King. (*rising*) My words fly up, my thoughts remain below:
Words without thoughts never to heaven go.   *Exit*

Scene IV

The Queen's closet

Enter Queen and Polonius

Polonius. 'A will come straight; look you lay home to him,
Tell him his pranks have been too broad to bear with,
And that your grace hath screen'd and stood between
Much heat and him. I'll silence me even here.
Pray you, be round {with him.
Hamlet. (*within*) Mother, mother, mother!}
Queen.   I'll warrant you; fear me not
Withdraw, I hear him coming.

Polonius hides behind the arras

Enter Hamlet

Hamlet. Now, mother, what's the matter?
Queen. Hamlet, thou hast thy father much offended.
Hamlet. Mother, you have my father much offended.
Queen. Come, come, you answer with an idle tongue.

Hamlet. Go, go, you question with a wicked tongue.

Queen. Why, how now, Hamlet?

Hamlet. What's the matter now?

Queen. Have you forgot me?

Hamlet. No, by the rood, not so:
   You are the queen, your husband's brother's wife,
   And would it were not so, you are my mother.

Queen. Nay, then, I'll set those to you that can speak.

Hamlet. Come, come, and sit you down; you shall not
      budge;
   You go not till I set you up a glass
   Where you may see the inmost part of you.

Queen. What wilt thou do? thou wilt not murder me?
   Help, ho!

Polonius. (*behind*) What, ho! help, {help, help!}

Hamlet. (*drawing*) How now! a rat? Dead for a ducat,
      dead!   *Makes a pass through the arras*

Polonius. (*behind*) O, I am slain!

Queen.   O me, what hast thou done?

Hamlet. Nay, I know not, is it the king?

Queen. O, what a rash and bloody deed is this!

Hamlet. A bloody deed; almost as bad, good mother,
   As kill a king, and marry with his brother.

Queen. As kill a king?

Hamlet.   Ay, lady, it was my word.
               Lifts up the arras and discovers Polonius
   Thou wretched, rash, intruding fool, farewell;
   I took thee for thy better; take thy fortune;
   Thou find'st to be too busy is some danger.
   Leave wringing of your hands: peace! sit you down,
   And let me wring your heart, for so I shall,
   If it be made of penetrable stuff,
   If damned custom have not brass'd it so,
   That it be proof and bulwark against sense.

Queen. What have I done, that thou dar'st wag thy tongue
   In noise so rude against me?

Hamlet.   Such an act
  That blurs the grace and blush of modesty,
  Calls virtue hypocrite, takes off the rose
  From the fair forehead of an innocent love,
  And sets a blister there, makes marriage vows
  As false as dicers' oaths, O, such a deed
  As from the body of contraction plucks
  The very soul, and sweet religion makes
  A rhapsody of words: heaven's face does glow
  O'er this solidity and compound mass,
  With heated visage, as against the doom
  Is thought-sick at the act.
Queen.   Ay me, what act,
  That roars so loud and thunders in the index?
Hamlet. Look here, upon this picture, and on this,
  The counterfeit presentment of two brothers.
  See what a grace was seated on this brow;
  Hyperion's curls, the front of Jove himself,
  An eye like Mars, to threaten and command,
  A station like the herald Mercury
  New-lighted on a heaven-kissing hill;
  A combination and a form indeed,
  Where every god did seem to set his seal
  To give the world assurance of a man:
  This was your husband. Look you now what follows:
  Here is your husband, like a mildew'd ear,
  Blasting his wholesome brother. Have you eyes?
  Could you on this fair mountain leave to feed,
  And batten on this moor? Ha! have you eyes?
  You cannot call it love, for at your age
  The hey-day in the blood is tame, it's humble,
  And waits upon the judgement, and what judgement
  Would step from this to this? [Sense sure you have,
  Else could you not have motion, but sure that sense
  Is apoplex'd, for madness would not err,
  Nor sense to ecstasy was ne'er so thrall'd

But it reserv'd some quantity of choice,
To serve in such a difference.] What devil was 't
That thus hath cozen'd you at hoodman-blind?
[Eyes without feeling, feeling without sight,
Ears without hands or eyes, smelling sans all,
Or but a sickly part of one true sense
Could not so mope.] O shame! where is thy blush?
Rebellious hell,
If thou canst mutine in a matron's bones,
To flaming youth let virtue be as wax
And melt in her own fire; proclaim no shame
When the compulsive ardour gives the charge,
Since frost itself as actively doth burn,
And reason pandars will.

Queen.   O Hamlet, speak no more:
Thou turn'st my very eyes into my soul,
And there I see such black and grained spots
As will leave there their tinct.

Hamlet.   Nay, but to live
In the rank sweat of an enseamed bed,
Stew'd in corruption, honeying and making love
Over the nasty sty,—

Queen.   O, speak to me no more;
These words like daggers enter in my ears;
No more, sweet Hamlet!

Hamlet.   A murderer and a villain,
A slave that is not twentieth part the tithe
Of your precedent lord, a Vice of kings,
A cutpurse of the empire and the rule,
That from a shelf the precious diadem stole
And put it in his pocket!

Queen.   No more!

Hamlet. A king of shreds and patches—

Enter Ghost

Save me and hover o'er me with your wings,
You heavenly guards! What would your gracious figure?

Queen. Alas, he's mad!

Hamlet. Do you not come your tardy son to chide,
That, laps'd in time and passion, lets go by
The important acting of your dread command?
O, say!

Ghost. Do not forget: this visitation
Is but to whet thy almost blunted purpose.
But look, amazement on thy mother sits;
O, step between her and her fighting soul:
Conceit in weakest bodies strongest works,
Speak to her, Hamlet.

Hamlet.   How is it with you, lady?

Queen. Alas, how is 't with you,
That you do bend your eye on vacancy,
And with the incorporal air do hold discourse?
Forth at your eyes your spirits wildly peep,
And, as the sleeping soldiers in the alarm,
Your bedded hair, like life in excrements,
Start up and stand an end. O gentle son,
Upon the heat and flame of thy distemper
Sprinkle cool patience. Whereon do you look?

Hamlet. On him, on him. Look you how pale he glares!
His form and cause conjoin'd, preaching to stones,
Would make them capable. Do not look upon me,
Lest with this piteous action you convert
My stern effects: then what I have to do
Will want true colour; tears perchance for blood.

Queen. To whom do you speak this?

Hamlet.   Do you see nothing there?

Queen. Nothing at all; yet all that is I see.

Hamlet. Nor did you nothing hear?

Queen.   No, nothing but ourselves.

Hamlet. Why, look you there! look, how it steals away!
My father, in his habit as he liv'd!
Look, where he goes, even now out at the portal!

Exit Ghost

Queen. This is the very coinage of your brain:
This bodiless creation ecstasy
Is very cunning in.
Hamlet.   {Ecstasy!}
My pulse, as yours, doth temperately keep time,
And makes as healthful music: it is not madness
That I have utter'd; bring me to the test,
And I the matter will re-word, which madness
Would gambol from. Mother, for love of grace,
Lay not that flattering unction to your soul,
That not your trespass but my madness speaks,
It will but skin and film the ulcerous place,
Whiles rank corruption, mining all within,
Infects unseen. Confess yourself to heaven,
Repent what's past, avoid what is to come,
And do not spread the compost on the weeds
To make them ranker. Forgive me this my virtue:
For in the fatness of these pursy times
Virtue itself of vice must pardon beg,
Yea, curb and woo for leave to do him good.
Queen. O Hamlet, thou hast cleft my heart in twain.
Hamlet. O, throw away the worser part of it,
And live the purer with the other half.
Good night: but go not to my uncle's bed;
Assume a virtue, if you have it not.
[That monster, custom, who all sense doth eat,
Of habits devil, is angel yet in this,
That to the use of actions fair and good
He likewise gives a frock or livery,
That aptly is put on.] Refrain to-night,
And that shall lend a kind of easiness
To the next abstinence; [the next more easy;
For use almost can change the stamp of nature,
And either . . . the devil, or throw him out
With wondrous potency.] Once more, good night:
And when you are desirous to be blest,

I'll blessing beg of you. For this same lord,

Pointing to Polonius

I do repent: but heaven hath pleas'd it so
To punish me with this, and this with me,
That I must be their scourge and minister.
I will bestow him, and will answer well
The death I gave him. So, again, good night;
I must be cruel, only to be kind:
This bad begins, and worse remains behind.
[One word more, good lady.]

Queen.   What shall I do?

Hamlet. Not this, by no means, that I bid you do:
Let the blowt king tempt you again to bed,
Pinch wanton on your cheek, call you his mouse,
And let him, for a pair of reechy kisses,
Or paddling in your neck with his damn'd fingers,
Make you to ravel all this matter out,
That I essentially am not in madness,
But mad in craft; 'twere good you let him know;
For who, that's but a queen, fair, sober, wise,
Would from a paddock, from a bat, a gib,
Such dear concernings hide! who would do so?
No, in despite of sense and secrecy,
Unpeg the basket on the house's top,
Let the birds fly, and like the famous ape,
To try conclusions, in the basket creep
And break your own neck down.

Queen. Be thou assur'd, if words be made of breath
And breath of life, I have no life to breathe
What thou hast said to me.

Hamlet. I must to England; you know that?

Queen.   Alack,
I had forgot: 'tis so concluded on.

Hamlet. [There's letters seal'd: and my two schoolfellows,
Whom I will trust as I will adders fang'd,
They bear the mandate; they must sweep my way,
And marshal me to knavery. Let it work;
For 'tis the sport to have the enginer
Hoist with his own petar, and 't shall go hard

But I will delve one yard below their mines,
And blow them at the moon: O, 'tis most sweet
When in one line two crafts directly meet.]
This man shall set me packing:
I'll lug the guts into the neighbour room.
Mother, good night indeed: this counsellor
Is now most still, most secret, and most grave,
Who was in life a most foolish prating knave.
Come, sir, to draw toward an end with you.
Good night, mother.

Exeunt severally; Hamlet dragging in Polonius

W.G. SIMMONDS

Act Four

Scene I

A room in the castle

Enter King, Queen, Rosencrantz, and Guildenstern

King. There's matter in these sighs, these profound heaves;
 You must translate, 'tis fit we understand them.
 Where is your son?
Queen. [Bestow this place on us a little while.]
                     Exeunt Rosencrantz and Guildenstern
 Ah, mine own lord, what have I seen to-night!
King. What, Gertrude? How does Hamlet?
Queen. Mad as the sea and wind when both contend
 Which is the mightier, in his lawless fit,
 Behind the arras hearing something stir,
 Whips out his rapier, cries 'A rat, a rat!'
 And in this brainish apprehension kills
 The unseen good old man.
King.   O heavy deed!

It had been so with us, had we been there;
His liberty is full of threats to all,
To you yourself, to us, to every one;
Alas, how shall this bloody deed be answer'd?
It will be laid to us, whose providence
Should have kept short, restrain'd, and out of haunt,
This mad young man: but so much was our love,
We would not understand what was most fit,
But, like the owner of a foul disease,
To keep it from divulging, let it feed
Even on the pith of life. Where is he gone?
Queen. To draw apart the body he hath kill'd:
O'er whom his very madness, like some ore
Among a mineral of metals base,
Shows itself pure; 'a weeps for what is done.
King. O Gertrude, come away!
The sun no sooner shall the mountains touch,
But we will ship him hence: and this vile deed
We must, with all our majesty and skill,
Both countenance and excuse. Ho, Guildenstern!

Re-enter Rosencrantz and Guildenstern

Friends both, go join you with some further aid;
Hamlet in madness hath Polonius slain,
And from his mother's closet hath he dragg'd him:
Go seek him out, speak fair, and bring the body
Into the chapel. I pray you, haste in this.

Exeunt Rosencrantz and Guildenstern

Come, Gertrude, we'll call up our wisest friends,
And let them know both what we mean to do
And what's untimely done. . . . .
[Whose whisper o'er the world's diameter
As level as the cannon to his blank
Transports his poison'd shot, may miss our name
And hit the woundless air.] O, come away!
My soul is full of discord and dismay.   *Exeunt*

Scene II

Another room in the castle

Enter Hamlet

Hamlet. Safely stow'd.

{Rosencrantz. ⎫
{Guildenstern. ⎬ (*within*) Hamlet! Lord Hamlet.}

Hamlet. [But soft,] what noise? who calls on Hamlet?
O, here they come.

Enter Rosencrantz and Guildenstern

Rosencrantz. What have you done, my lord, with the dead
body?

Hamlet. Compounded it with dust, whereto 'tis kin.

Rosencrantz. Tell us where 'tis, that we may take it thence,
And bear it to the chapel.

Hamlet. Do not believe it.

Rosencrantz. Believe what?

Hamlet. That I can keep your counsel and not mine own.
Besides, to be demanded of a sponge, what replication
should be made by the son of a king?

Rosencrantz. Take you me for a sponge, my lord?

Hamlet. Ay, sir; that soaks up the king's countenance, his
rewards, his authorities. But such officers do the king
best service in the end: he keeps them, like an ape, in the
corner of his jaw, first mouth'd, to be last swallow'd: when
he needs what you have glean'd, it is but squeezing you,
and, sponge, you shall be dry again.

Rosencrantz. I understand you not, my lord.

Hamlet. I am glad of it: a knavish speech sleeps in a foolish
ear.

Rosencrantz. My lord, you must tell us where the body is,
and go with us to the king.

Hamlet. The body is with the king, but the king is not with
the body. The king is a thing—

Guildenstern. A thing, my lord?

Hamlet. Of nothing: bring me to him. {Hide fox, and all after.}   *Exeunt*

Scene III

Another room in the castle

Enter King, attended

King. I have sent to seek him, and to find the body.
How dangerous is it that this man goes loose!
Yet must not we put the strong law on him;
He's loved of the distracted multitude,
Who like not in their judgement, but their eyes;
And where 'tis so, the offender's scourge is weigh'd,
But never the offence. To bear all smooth and even,
This sudden sending him away must seem
Deliberate pause: diseases desperate grown
By desperate appliance are reliev'd,
Or not at all.

Enter Rosencrantz and others

How now! what hath befall'n?

Rosencrantz. Where the dead body is bestow'd, my lord,
We cannot get from him.

King.   But where is he?

Rosencrantz. Without, my lord, guarded to know your pleasure.

King. Bring him before us.

Rosencrantz. Ho, bring in the lord.

Enter Hamlet guarded

King. Now, Hamlet, where's Polonius?

Hamlet. At supper.

King. At supper, where?

Hamlet. Not where he eats, but where he is eaten: a certain convocation of politic worms are e'en at him. Your worm is your only emperor for diet: we fat all creatures else to fat us, and we fat ourselves for maggots: your fat king and your lean beggar is but variable service, two dishes, but to one table: that's the end.

[*King.* Alas, alas!

Hamlet. A man may fish with the worm that hath eat of a king, and eat of the fish that hath fed of that worm.]

King. What dost thou mean by this?

Hamlet. Nothing but to show you how a king may go a progress through the guts of a beggar.

King. Where is Polonius?

Hamlet. In heaven; send thither to see: if your messenger find him not there, seek him i' the other place yourself; but if indeed you find him not within this month, you shall nose him as you go up the stairs into the lobby.

King. Go seek him there.   *To some Attendants*

Hamlet. 'A will stay till you come.   *Exeunt Attendants*

King. Hamlet, this deed, for thine especial safety,
    Which we do tender, as we dearly grieve
    For that which thou hast done, must send thee hence
    {With fiery quickness}: therefore prepare thyself;
    The bark is ready, and the wind at help,
    The associates tend, and every thing is bent
    For England.

Hamlet.   For England?

King.   Ay, Hamlet.

Hamlet.   Good.

King. So is it, if thou knew'st our purposes.

Hamlet. I see a cherub that sees them. But, come, for England! Farewell, dear mother.

King. Thy loving father, Hamlet.

Hamlet. My mother; father and mother is man and wife,
man and wife is one flesh, so my mother. Come, for Eng-
land!   *Exit*
King. Follow him at foot, tempt him with speed aboard,
Delay it not; I'll have him hence to-night:
Away! for every thing is seal'd and done
That else leans on the affair: pray you, make haste;
                Exeunt Rosencrantz and Guildenstern
And, England, if my love thou hold'st at aught—
As my great power thereof may give thee sense,
Since yet thy cicatrice looks raw and red
After the Danish sword; and thy free awe
Pays homage to us, thou mayst not coldly set
Our sovereign process, which imports at full,
By letters congruing to that effect,
The present death of Hamlet. Do it, England;
For like the hectic in my blood he rages,
And thou must cure me: till I know 'tis done,
Howe'er my haps, my joys will ne'er begin.   *Exit*

Scene V

The next day

A plain in Denmark

Enter Fortinbras with his army over the stage

Fortinbras. Go, captain, from me greet the Danish king;
Tell him that by his licence Fortinbras
Craves the conveyance of a promis'd march
Over his kingdom. You know the rendezvous.
If that his majesty would aught with us,
We shall express our duty in his eye;
And let him know so.
Captain.   I will do 't, my lord.

Fortinbras. Go softly on. *Exeunt [Fortinbras and Soldiers*

Enter Hamlet, Rosencrantz, Guildenstern, and others

Hamlet. Good sir, whose powers are these?
Captain. They are of Norway, sir.
Hamlet. How purpos'd, sir, I pray you?
Captain. Against some part of Poland.
Hamlet. Who commands them, sir?
Captain. The nephew to old Norway, Fortinbras.
Hamlet. Goes it against the main of Poland, sir,
  Or for some frontier?
Captain. Truly to speak, and with no addition,
  We go to gain a little patch of ground
  That hath in it no profit but the name.
  To pay five ducats, five, I would not farm it;
  Nor will it yield to Norway or the Pole
  A ranker rate, should it be sold in fee.
Hamlet. Why then the Polack never will defend it.
Captain. Yet, it is already garrison'd.
Hamlet. Two thousand souls and twenty thousand ducats
  Will not debate the question of this straw:
  This is the imposthume of much wealth and peace,
  That inward breaks, and shows no cause without
  Why the man dies. I humbly thank you, sir.
Captain. God be wi' you, sir.   *Exit*
Rosencrantz.   Will 't please you go, my lord?
Hamlet. I'll be with you straight, go a little before.
                    Exeunt all but Hamlet
  How all occasions do inform against me,
  And spur my dull revenge! What is a man,
  If his chief good and market of his time
  Be but to sleep and feed? a beast, no more.
  Sure, he that made us with such large discourse,
  Looking before and after, gave us not
  That capability and god-like reason
  To fust in us unus'd. Now, whether it be
  Bestial oblivion, or some craven scruple

Of thinking too precisely on the event,—
A thought which, quarter'd, hath but one part wisdom
And ever three parts coward,—I do not know
Why yet I live to say 'this thing's to do,'
Sith I have cause, and will, and strength, and means
To do 't. Examples gross as earth exhort me;
Witness this army of such mass and charge,
Led by a delicate and tender prince,
Whose spirit with divine ambition puff'd
Makes mouths at the invisible event,
Exposing what is mortal and unsure
To all that fortune, death, and danger dare,
Even for an egg-shell. Rightly to be great
Is not to stir without great argument,
But greatly to find quarrel in a straw
When honour's at the stake. How stand I then,
That have a father kill'd, a mother stain'd,
Excitements of my reason and my blood,
And let all sleep, while to my shame I see
The imminent death of twenty thousand men,
That for a fantasy and trick of fame
Go to their graves like beds, fight for a plot
Whereon the numbers cannot try the cause,
Which is not tomb enough and continent
To hide the slain? O, from this time forth,
My thoughts be bloody, or be nothing worth!   *Exit*]

Scene V

A few days later

Elsinore. A room in the castle

Enter Queen, Horatio, [and a Gentleman]

Queen. I will not speak with her.
Gentleman. She is importunate, indeed distract:
  Her mood will needs be pitied.
Queen.   What would she have?
Gentleman. She speaks much of her father, says she hears
  There's tricks i' the world, and hems and beats her heart,
  Spurns enviously at straws, speaks things in doubt,
  That carry but half sense: her speech is nothing,
  Yet the unshaped use of it doth move
  The hearers to collection; they aim at it,
  And botch the words up fit to their own thoughts;
  Which, as her winks, and nods, and gestures yield them,
  Indeed would make one think there might be thought,
  Though nothing sure, yet much unhappily.
Horatio. 'Twere good she were spoken with, for she may strew
  Dangerous conjectures in ill-breeding minds.
  Let her come in.   *Exit Gentleman*
Queen. (*aside*) To my sick soul, as sin's true nature is,
  Each toy seems prologue to some great amiss:
  So full of artless jealousy is guilt,
  It spills itself in fearing to be spilt.

Enter Ophelia

Ophelia. Where is the beauteous majesty of Denmark?
Queen. How now, Ophelia?
Ophelia. (*sings*) How should I your true love know
                  From another one?
              By his cockle hat and staff
              And his sandal shoon.
Queen. Alas, sweet lady, what imports this song?

Ophelia. Say you? nay, pray you, mark.

> (*sings*) He is dead and gone, lady,
> > He is dead and gone,
> > At his head a grass-green turf,
> > At his heels a stone.

O ho!

Queen. Nay, but Ophelia,—

Ophelia.   Pray you, mark.

> (*sings*) White his shroud as the mountain snow,—

Enter King

Queen. Alas, look here, my lord.

Ophelia. (*sings*)   Larded all with sweet flowers;

> > Which bewept to the grave did not go
> > With true-love showers.

King. How do you, pretty lady?

Ophelia. Well, God 'ild you! They say the owl was a baker's daughter; Lord, we know what we are, but know not what we may be. God be at your table!

King. Conceit upon her father.

Ophelia. Pray, let's have no words of this, but when they ask you what it means, say you this:

> (*sings*) To-morrow is Saint Valentine's day,
> > All in the morning betime,
> > And I a maid at your window,
> > To be your Valentine.
> > Then up he rose, and donn'd his clo'es,
> > And dupp'd the chamber-door,
> > Let in the maid, that out a maid
> > Never departed more.

King. Pretty Ophelia!

Ophelia. Indeed, without an oath, I'll make an end on 't:

> (*sings*) By Gis and by Saint Charity,
> > Alack, and fie for shame!
> > Young men will do 't, if they come to 't,
> > By cock, they are to blame.
> > Quoth she, before you tumbled me,
> > You promised me to wed.

He answers:
> So would I ha' done, by yonder sun,
> An thou hadst not come to my bed.

King. How long hath she been thus?

Ophelia. I hope all will be well, we must be patient, but I cannot choose but weep to think they would lay him i' the cold ground, my brother shall know of it, and so I thank you for your good counsel. Come, my coach! Good night, ladies, good night; sweet ladies, good night, good night.   *Exit*

King. Follow her close, give her good watch, I pray you.
                                                                        Exit Horatio

> O, this is the poison of deep grief; it springs
> All from her father's death, and now behold!
> O Gertrude, Gertrude,
> When sorrows come, they come not single spies,
> But in battalions. First, her father slain;
> Next, your son gone, and he most violent author
> Of his own just remove; the people muddied,
> Thick and unwholesome in their thoughts, and whispers
> For good Polonius' death: and we have done but greenly,
> In hugger-mugger to inter him: poor Ophelia
> Divided from herself, and her fair judgement,
> Without the which we are pictures, or mere beasts;
> Last, and as much containing as all these,
> Her brother is in secret come from France,
> Feeds on this wonder, keeps himself in clouds,
> And wants not buzzers to infect his ear
> With pestilent speeches of his father's death;
> Wherein necessity, of matter beggar'd,
> Will nothing stick our person to arraign
> In ear and ear. O my dear Gertrude, this,
> Like to a murdering-piece, in many places
> Gives me superfluous death.   *A noise within*

{*Queen.*   Alack, what noise is this?}

King. Attend, where are my Switzers? Let them guard the door.

Enter a Messenger

What is the matter?
Messenger.　　　　Save yourself, my lord:
　The ocean, overpeering of his list,
　Eats not the flats with more impiteous haste
　Than young Laertes in a riotous head
　O'erbears your officers: the rabble call him lord;
　And, as the world were now but to begin,
　Antiquity forgot, custom not known,
　The ratifiers and props of every word,
　They cry 'Choose we; Laertes shall be king!'
　Caps, hands and tongues applaud it to the clouds,
　'Laertes shall be king, Laertes king!'
Queen. How cheerfully on the false trail they cry!
　　　　　　　　　　　　　　Noise within
　O, this is counter, you false Danish dogs!
King. The doors are broke.

Enter Laertes, armed; Danes following

Laertes. Where is this king? Sirs, stand you all without.
Danes. No, let's come in.
Laertes.　　　　　　I pray you, give me leave.
Danes. We will, we will.　*They retire without the door*
Laertes. I thank you: keep the door. O thou vile king,
　Give me my father!
Queen.　　　　　Calmly, good Laertes.
Laertes. That drop of blood that's calm proclaims me bas-
　　tard,
　Cries cuckold to my father, brands the harlot
　Even here, between the chaste unsmirched brow
　Of my true mother.
King.　　　　　What is the cause, Laertes,
　That thy rebellion looks so giant-like?
　Let him go, Gertrude; do not fear our person:

There's such divinity doth hedge a king,
That treason can but peep to what it would,
Acts little of his will. Tell me, Laertes,
Why thou art thus incens'd: let him go, Gertrude:
Speak, man.
Laertes. Where is my father?
King.   Dead.
Queen.   But not by him.
King. Let him demand his fill.
Laertes. How came he dead? I'll not be juggled with:
To hell, allegiance! vows, to the blackest devil!
Conscience and grace, to the profoundest pit!
I dare damnation: to this point I stand,
That both the worlds I give to negligence,
Let come what comes; only I'll be reveng'd
Most throughly for my father.
King.   Who shall stay you?
Laertes. My will, not all the world's:
And for my means, I'll husband them so well,
They shall go far with little.
King.   Good Laertes,
If you desire to know the certainty
Of your dear father, is 't writ in your revenge
That, swoopstake, you will draw both friend and foe,
Winner and loser?
Laertes. None but his enemies.
King.   Will you know them then?
Laertes. To his good friends thus wide I'll ope my arms;
And, like the kind life-rendering pelican,
Repast them with my blood.
King.   Why, now you speak
Like a good child and a true gentleman.
That I am guiltless of your father's death,
And am most sensibly in grief for it,
It shall as level to your judgement 'pear
As day does to your eye.

Danes. (*within*) Let her come in.
Laertes. How now, what noise is that?

Re-enter Ophelia

O heat, dry up my brains! tears seven times salt,
Burn out the sense and virtue of mine eye!
By heaven, thy madness shall be paid with weight,
Till our scale turn the beam. O rose of May,
Dear maid, kind sister, sweet Ophelia!
O heavens! is 't possible a young maid's wits
Should be as mortal as an old man's life?
{Nature is fine in love, and where 'tis fine
It sends some precious instance of itself
After the thing it loves.}
Ophelia. (*sings*) They bore him barefac'd on the bier:
{Hey non nonny, nonny, hey nonney:}
And in his grave rain'd many a tear,—
Fare you well, my dove!
Laertes. Hadst thou thy wits, and didst persuade revenge,
It could not move thus.
Ophelia. (*sings*) You must sing a-down a-down,
An you call him a-down-a.
O, how the wheel becomes it! It is the false steward that
stole his master's daughter.
Laertes. This nothing's more than matter.
Ophelia. There's rosemary, that's for remembrance; pray
you, love, remember; and there is pansies, that's for
thoughts.
Laertes. A document in madness, thoughts and remembrance fitted.
Ophelia. There's fennel for you, and columbines, there's rue
for you, and here's some for me, we may call it herb of
grace o' Sundays, you may wear your rue with a difference, there's a daisy, I would give you some violets, but
they wither'd all when my father died, they say 'a made a
good end,
(*sings*) For bonnie sweet Robin is all my joy.

Laertes. Thought and afflictions, passion, hell itself,
  She turns to favour and to prettiness.
Ophelia. (*sings*) And will 'a not come again?
                    And will 'a not come again?
                      No, no, he is dead,
                      Go to thy death-bed,
                    He never will come again.
                    His beard was as white as snow,
                    Flaxen was his poll:
                      He is gone, he is gone,
                      And we cast away moan,
                    God ha' mercy on his soul!
  And of all Christian souls, {I pray God.} God be wi' you.
                                                        Exit

Laertes. Do you see this, O God?
King. Laertes, I must commune with your grief,
  Or you deny me right. Go but apart,
  Make choice of whom your wisest friends you will,
  And they shall hear and judge 'twixt you and me;
  If by direct or by collateral hand
  They find us touch'd, we will our kingdom give,
  Our crown, our life, and all that we call ours,
  To you in satisfaction; but if not,
  Be you content to lend your patience to us,
  And we shall jointly labour with your soul
  To give it due content.
Laertes.   Let this be so.
  His means of death, his obscure funeral,
  No trophy, sword, nor hatchment o'er his bones,
  No noble rite, nor formal ostentation,
  Cry to be heard, as 'twere from heaven to earth,
  That I must call 't in question.
King.   So you shall;
  And where the offence is, let the great axe fall.
  I pray you, go with me.   *Exeunt*

Scene VI

Another room in the castle

Enter Horatio and a Servant

Horatio. What are they that would speak with me?

Servant. Sea-faring men, sir: they say they have letters for you.

Horatio. Let them come in.　　　　　　　*Exit Servant*

I do not know from what part of the world
I should be greeted; if not from Lord Hamlet.

Enter Sailors

First Sail. God bless you, sir.

Horatio. Let him bless thee too.

First Sail. 'A shall, sir, an please him. There's a letter for you, sir, it came from the ambassador that was bound for England, if your name be Horatio, as I am let to know it is.

Horatio. (*reads*) 'Horatio, when thou shalt have overlook'd this, give these fellows some means to the king: they have letters for him. Ere we were two days old at sea, a pirate of very warlike appointment gave us chase; finding ourselves too slow of sail, we put on a compell'd valour, and in the grapple I boarded them, on the instant they got clear of our ship, so I alone became their prisoner. They have dealt with me like thieves of mercy, but they knew what they did; I am to do a turn for them. Let the king have the letters I have sent, and repair thou to me with as much speed as thou wouldest fly death; I have words to speak in thine ear will make thee dumb, yet are they much too light for the bore of the matter. These good fellows will bring thee where I am. Rosencrantz and Guildenstern hold their course for England: of them I have much to tell thee. Farewell.

　　　　　　　'He that thou knowest thine HAMLET.

Come, I will give you way for these your letters
And do 't the speedier, that you may direct me
To him from whom you brought them.　　　　*Exeunt*

Scene VII

Another room in the castle

Enter King and Laertes

King. Now must your conscience my acquittance seal,
And you must put me in your heart for friend,
Sith you have heard, and with a knowing ear,
That he which hath your noble father slain
Pursued my life.
Laertes.   It well appears: but tell me
Why you proceeded not against these feats,
So criminal and so capital in nature,
As by your safety, wisdom, all things else,
You mainly were stirr'd up.
King.   O, for two special reasons,
Which may to you perhaps seem much unsinew'd,
But yet to me they're strong. The queen his mother
Lives almost by his looks; and for myself—
My virtue or my plague, be it either which—
She's so conjunctive to my life and soul,
That, as the star moves not but in his sphere,
I could not but by her. The other motive,
Why to a public count I might not go,
Is the great love the general gender bear him;
Who, dipping all his faults in their affection,
Work, like the spring that turneth wood to stone,
Convert his gyves to graces, so that my arrows,
Too slightly timber'd for so loud a wind,
Would have reverted to my bow again
But not where I have aim'd them.
Laertes. And so have I a noble father lost;
A sister driven into desperate terms,
Whose worth, if praises may go back again,
Stood challenger on mount of all the age
For her perfections: but my revenge will come.
King. Break not your sleeps for that: you must not think
That we are made of stuff so flat and dull
That we can let our beard be shook with danger,

And think it pastime. You shortly shall hear more:
I lov'd your father, and we love ourself;
And that, I hope, will teach you to imagine—

Enter a Messenger, with letters

{How now! what news?
Messenger.   Letters, my lord, from Hamlet:}
These to your majesty; this to the queen.
King. From Hamlet? who brought them?
Messenger. Sailors, my lord, they say; I saw them not:
They were given me by Claudio; he receiv'd them
Of him that brought them.
King.   Laertes, you shall hear them.
Leave us.   *Exit Messenger*
(*reads*) 'High and mighty, you shall know I am set naked
on your kingdom. To-morrow shall I beg leave to see
your kingly eyes, when I shall, first asking you pardon,
there unto recount the occasion of my sudden {and more
strange} return.

{'HAMLET.'}

What should this mean? Are all the rest come back?
Or is it some abuse, and no such thing?
Laertes. Know you the hand?
King. 'Tis Hamlet's character. 'Naked'!
And in a postscript here, he says 'alone':
Can you devise me?
Laertes. I am lost in it, my lord. But let him come;
It warms the very sickness in my heart,
That I shall live and tell him to his teeth,
'Thus didst thou.'
King.   If it be so, Laertes,—
As how should it be so? how otherwise?—
Will you be ruled by me?
Laertes.   [Ay, my lord;]
So you will not o'errule me to a peace.
King. To thine own peace. If he be now return'd,

As checking at his voyage, and that he means
No more to undertake it, I will work him
To an exploit now ripe in my device,
Under the which he shall not choose but fall:
And for his death no wind of blame shall breathe,
But even his mother shall uncharge the practice,
And call it accident.
[*Laertes.*　　　　　My lord, I will be rul'd;
　The rather, if you could devise it so
　That I might be the organ.
King.　　　　　It falls right.
　You have been talk'd of since your travel much,
　And that in Hamlet's hearing, for a quality
　Wherein they say you shine: your sum of parts
　Did not together pluck such envy from him,
　As did that one, and that in my regard
　Of the unworthiest siege.
Laertes.　　　　　What part is that, my lord?
King. A very riband in the cap of youth,
　Yet needful too; for youth no less becomes
　The light and careless livery that it wears
　Than settled age his sables and his weeds,
　Importing health and graveness.] Two months since,
　Here was a gentleman of Normandy:—
　I've seen myself, and serv'd against, the French,
　And they can well on horseback: but this gallant
　Had witchcraft in 't; he grew unto his seat,
　And to such wondrous doing brought his horse
　As had he been incorps'd, and demi-natur'd
　With the brave beast: so far he topp'd my thought
　That I, in forgery of shapes and tricks,
　Come short of what he did.
Laertes.　　　　　A Norman was 't?
King. A Norman.
Laertes. Upon my life, Lamond.
King.　　　　　The very same.
Laertes. I know him well: he is the brooch indeed
　And gem of all the nation.

King. He made confession of you,
  And gave you such a masterly report
  For art and exercise in your defence,
  And for your rapier most especial,
  That he cried out, 'twould be a sight indeed
  If one could match you: [the scrimers of their nation,
  He swore, had neither motion, guard, nor eye,
  If you oppos'd them.] Sir, this report of his
  Did Hamlet so envenom with his envy
  That he could nothing do but wish and beg
  Your sudden coming o'er, to play with you.
  Now, out of this—
Laertes.   What out of this, my lord?
King. Laertes, was your father dear to you?
  Or are you like the painting of a sorrow,
  A face without a heart?
Laertes.   Why ask you this?
King. Not that I think you did not love your father,
  But that I know love is begun by time,
  And that I see, in passages of proof,
  Time qualifies the spark and fire of it.
  [There lives within the very flame of love
  A kind of wick or snuff that will abate it;
  And nothing is at a like goodness still,
  For goodness, growing to a plurisy,
  Dies in his own too much: that we would do
  We should do when we would; for this 'would' changes
  And hath abatements and delays as many
  As there are tongues, are hands, are accidents,
  And then this 'should' is like a spendthrift's sigh,
  That hurts by easing. But, to the quick o' the ulcer:]
  Hamlet comes back: what would you undertake,
  To show yourself indeed your father's son
  More than in words?
Laertes.   To cut his throat i' the church.
King. No place indeed should murder sanctuarize;
  Revenge should have no bounds. But, good Laertes,

Will you do this, keep close within your chamber.
Hamlet return'd shall know you are come home:
We'll put on those shall praise your excellence
And set a double varnish on the fame
The Frenchman gave you; bring you in fine together
And wager o'er your heads: he, being remiss,
Most generous, and free from all contriving,
Will not peruse the foils, so that with ease,
Or with a little shuffling, you may choose
A sword unbated, and in a pass of practice
Requite him for your father.

Laertes.   I will do 't;
And for that purpose I'll anoint my sword.
I bought an unction of a mountebank,
So mortal, that but dip a knife in it,
Where it draws blood, no cataplasm so rare,
Collected from all simples that have virtue
Under the moon, can save the thing from death
That is but scratch'd withal: I'll touch my point
With this contagion, that, if I gall him slightly,
It may be death.

King.   Let's further think of this;
Weigh what convenience both of time and means
May fit us to our shape: if this should fail,
And that our drift look through our bad performance,
'Twere better not assay'd: therefore this project
Should have a back or second, that might hold
If this did blast in proof. Soft! let me see:
We'll make a solemn wager on your cunnings:
I ha 't:
When in your motion you are hot and dry—
As make your bouts more violent to that end—
And that he calls for drink, I'll have prepar'd him
A chalice for the nonce, whereon but sipping,
If he by chance escape your venom'd stuck,
Our purpose may hold there. [But stay, what noise?]

Enter Queen

[How now, sweet queen?]

Queen. One woe doth tread upon another's heel,
So fast they follow: your sister's drown'd, Laertes.

Laertes. Drown'd! O, where?

Queen. There is a willow grows ascaunt the brook,
That shows his hoar leaves in the glassy stream;
Therewith fantastic garlands did she make
Of crow-flowers, nettles, daisies, and long purples,
That liberal shepherds give a grosser name,
But our cold maids do dead men's fingers call them:
There, on the pendent boughs her crownet weeds
Clambering to hang, an envious sliver broke,
When down her weedy trophies and herself
Fell in the weeping brook, her clothes spread wide,
And mermaid-like a while they bore her up:
Which time she chanted snatches of old lauds,
As one incapable of her own distress,
Or like a creature native and indued
Unto that element: but long it could not be
Till that her garments, heavy with their drink,
Pull'd the poor wretch from her melodious lay
To muddy death.

Laertes.   Alas, then she is drown'd!

Queen. Drown'd, drown'd.

Laertes. Too much of water hast thou, poor Ophelia,
And therefore I forbid my tears: but yet
It is our trick: nature her custom holds,
Let shame say what it will: when these are gone,
The woman will be out. Adieu, my lord:
I have a speech afire that fain would blaze,
But that this folly douts it.   *Exit*

King.   Let's follow, Gertrude:
How much I had to do to calm his rage!
Now fear I this will give it start again;
Therefore let's follow.   *Exeunt*

Act Five

Scene I

The next day

A churchyard

Enter two Clowns, with spades, &c.

First Clown. Is she to be buried in Christian burial when she wilfully seeks her own salvation?

Sec. Clown. I tell thee she is; therefore make her grave straight: the crowner hath sat on her, and finds it Christian burial.

First Clown. How can that be, unless she drown'd herself in her own defence?

Sec. Clown. Why, 'tis found so.

First Clown. It must be 'so offended;' it cannot be else. For here lies the point: if I drown myself wittingly, it argues an act: and an act hath three branches; it is, to act, to do, to perform, argal she drown'd herself wittingly.

Sec. Clown. Nay, but hear you, goodman delver.

First Clown. Give me leave. Here lies the water; good: here stands the man; good: if the man go to this water and drown himself, it is, will he, nill he, he goes, mark you that; but if the water come to him and drown him, he drowns not himself: argal, he that is not guilty of his own death shortens not his own life.

Sec. Clown. But is this law?

First Clown. Ay, marry, is 't; crowner's quest law.

Sec. Clown. Will you ha' the truth on 't? If this had not been a gentlewoman, she should have been buried out o' Christian burial.

First Clown. Why, there thou say'st: and the more pity that great folk should have countenance in this world to drown or hang themselves, more than their even Christian. Come, my spade; there is no ancient gentlemen but gardeners, ditchers, and grave-makers: they hold up Adam's profession.

Sec. Clown. Was he a gentleman?

First Clown. 'A was the first that ever bore arms.

{*Sec. Clown.* Why, he had none.

First Clown. What, art a heathen? How dost thou understand the Scripture? The Scripture says Adam digg'd: could he dig without arms?} I'll put another question to thee: if thou answerest me not to the purpose, confess thyself—

Sec. Clown. Go to.

First Clown. What is he that builds stronger than either the mason, the shipwright, or the carpenter?

Sec. Clown. The gallows-maker; for that outlives a thousand tenants.

First Clown. I like thy wit well, in good faith: the gallows does well; but how does it well? it does well to those that do ill: now, thou dost ill to say the gallows is built stronger than the chuuch: argal, the gallows may do well to thee. To 't again, come.

Sec. Clown. 'Who builds stronger than a mason, a shipwright, or a carpenter?'

First Clown. Ay, tell me that, and unyoke.

Sec. Clown. Marry, now I can tell.

First Clown. To 't.

Sec. Clown. Mass, I cannot tell.

First Clown. Cudgel thy brains no more about it, for your dull ass will not mend his pace with beating, and when you are ask'd this question next, say 'a grave-maker: the houses he makes lasts till doomsday.' Go, get thee in, and fetch me a stoup of liquor.　　　　*Exit Sec. Clown.*

He digs, and sings

> In youth, when I did love, did love,
>   Methought it was very sweet
> To contract, O, the time, for-a my behove,
>   O, methought, there-a was nothing-a meet.

Enter Hamlet and Horatio

Hamlet. Has this fellow no feeling of his business? 'A sings in grave-making.

Horatio. Custom hath made it in him a property of easiness.

Hamlet. 'Tis e'en so: the hand of little employment hath the daintier sense.

First Clown. (*sings*) But age, with his stealing steps
     Hath clawed me in his clutch,
     And hath shipped me into the land,
     As if I had never been such.
          Throws up a skull

Hamlet. That skull had a tongue in it, and could sing once: how the knave jowls it to the ground, as if 'twere Cain's jaw-bone, that did the first murder! This might be the pate of a politician, which this ass now o'er-reaches; one that would circumvent God, might it not?

Horatio. It might, my lord.

Hamlet. Or of a courtier, which could say 'Good morrow, sweet lord? How dost thou, sweet lord?' This might be my lord such-a-one, that prais'd my lord such-a-one's horse, when 'a went to beg it, might it not?

Horatio. Ay, my lord.

Hamlet. Why, e'en so: and now my Lady Worm's, chopless, and knocked about the mazzard with a sexton's spade: here's fine revolution, an we had the trick to see 't; did these bones cost no more the breeding, but to play at loggits with them? mine ache to think on 't.

First Clown. (*sings*) A pick-axe, and a spade, a spade,
     For and a shrouding sheet:
     O, a pit of clay for to be made
     For such a guest is meet.
        Throws up another skull

Hamlet. There's another: why may not that be the skull of a lawyer? Where be his quiddities now, his quillets, his cases, his tenures, and his tricks? why does he suffer this mad knave now to knock him about the sconce with a dirty shovel, and will not tell him of his action of battery? Hum! This fellow might be in 's time a great buyer of

land, with his statutes, his recognizances, his fines, his
double vouchers, his recoveries: {is this the fine of his
fines and the recovery of his recoveries,} to have his fine
pate full of fine dirt? will vouchers vouch him no more of
his purchases, and doubles, than the length and breadth
of a pair of indentures? The very conveyances of his lands
will scarcely lie in this box, and must the inheritor himself have no more, ha?

Horatio. Not a jot more, my lord.

Hamlet. Is not parchment made of sheep-skins?

Horatio. Ay, my lord, and of calves-skins too.

Hamlet. They are sheep and calves which seek out assurance in that. I will speak to this fellow. Whose grave's
this, sirrah?

First Clown. Mine, sir.

(*sings*) Or a pit of clay for to be made
{For such a guest is meet.}

Hamlet. I think it be thine indeed, for thou liest in 't.

First Clown. You lie out on 't, sir, and therefore 'tis not
yours: for my part, I do not lie in 't, and yet it is mine.

Hamlet. Thou dost lie in 't, to be in 't and say it is thine:
'tis for the dead, not for the quick; therefore thou liest.

First Clown. 'Tis a quick lie, sir; 'twill away again from me
to you.

Hamlet. What man dost thou dig it for?

First Clown. For no man, sir.

Hamlet. What woman then?

First Clown. For none neither.

Hamlet. Who is to be buried in 't?

First Clown. One that was a woman, sir; but, rest her soul,
she's dead.

Hamlet. How absolute the knave is! we must speak by the
card, or equivocation will undo us. By the Lord, Horatio,
this three years I have took note of it, the age is grown
so pick'd, that the toe of the peasant comes so near the

heel of the courtier, he galls his kibe. How long hast thou
been grave-maker?

First Clown. Of the days i' the year I came to 't that day
that our last king Hamlet overcame Fortinbras.

Hamlet. How long is that since?

First Clown. Cannot you tell that? every fool can tell that:
it was that very day that young Hamlet was born: he
that is mad, and sent into England.

Hamlet. Ay, marry, why was he sent into England?

First Clown. Why, because 'a was mad; 'a shall recover his
wits there; or, if 'a do not, 'tis no great matter there.

Hamlet. Why?

First Clown. 'Twill not be seen in him there; there the men
are as mad as he.

Hamlet. How came he mad?

First Clown. Very strangely, they say.

Hamlet. How 'strangely'?

First Clown. Faith, e'en with losing his wits.

Hamlet. Upon what ground?

First Clown. Why, here in Denmark: I have been sexton
here, man and boy, thirty years.

Hamlet. How long will a man lie i' the earth ere he rot?

First Clown. I' faith if 'a be not rotten before 'a die—as we
have many pocky corses {now-a-days,} that will scarce
hold the laying in—'a will last you some eight year or nine
year: a tanner will last you nine year.

Hamlet. Why he more than another?

First Clown. Why, sir, his hide is so tann'd with his trade
that 'a will keep out water a great while; and your water
is a sore decayer of your whoreson dead body. Here's a
skull now hath lien you i' the earth three and twenty
years.

Hamlet. Whose was it?

First Clown. A whoreson mad fellow's it was; whose do
you think it was?

Hamlet. Nay, I know not.

First Clown. A pestilence on him for a mad rogue! 'a pour'd a flagon of Rhenish on my head once. This same skull, sir, was, sir, Yorick's skull, the king's jester.

Hamlet. This?

First Clown. E'en that.

Hamlet. {Let me see.} (*Takes the skull.*) Alas, poor Yorick! I knew him, Horatio, a fellow of infinite jest, of most excellent fancy: he hath borne me on his back a thousand times, and now how abhorred in my imagination it is! my gorge rises at it. Here hung those lips that I have kiss'd I know not how oft; where be your gibes now? your gambols, your songs, your flashes of merriment, that were wont to set the table on a roar? Not one now to mock your own grinning, quite chop-fallen. Now get you to my lady's table, and tell her, let her paint an inch thick, to this favour she must come; make her laugh at that. Prithee, Horatio, tell me one thing.

Horatio. What's that, my lord?

Hamlet. Dost thou think Alexander looked o' this fashion i' the earth?

Horatio. E'en so.

Hamlet. And smelt so? pah!   *Puts down the skull*

Horatio. E'en so, my lord.

Hamlet. To what base uses we may return, Horatio! Why may not imagination trace the noble dust of Alexander, till 'a find it stopping a bung-hole?

Horatio. 'Twere to consider too curiously, to consider so.

Hamlet. No, faith, not a jot; but to follow him thither with modesty enough, and likelihood to lead it: {as thus:} Alexander died, Alexander was buried, Alexander returneth to dust, the dust is earth, of earth we make loam, and why of that loam, whereto he was converted, might they not stop a beer-barrel?

Imperious Cæsar, dead and turn'd to clay,
Might stop a hole, to keep the wind away.
O, that that earth, which kept the world in awe,
Should patch a wall to expel the winter's flaw!

But soft! but soft, awhile: here comes the king.

Enter the Corpse of Ophelia, a Priest, King, Queen,
Laertes, Courtiers

The queen, the courtiers: who is this they follow?
And with such maimed rites? This doth betoken
The corse they follow did with desperate hand
Fordo its own life: 'twas of some estate.
Couch we awhile, and mark.   *Retiring with Horatio*
Laertes. What ceremony else?
Hamlet. That is Laertes, a very noble youth: mark.
Laertes. What ceremony else?
Priest. Her obsequies have been as far enlarg'd
As we have warranty: her death was doubtful,
And, but that great command o'ersways the order,
She should in ground unsanctified been lodg'd
Till the last trumpet; for charitable prayers,
{Shards,} flints and pebbles should be thrown on her:
Yet here she is allow'd her virgin crants,
Her maiden strewments, and the bringing home
Of bell and burial.
Laertes. Must there no more be done?
Priest.   No more be done:
We should profane the service of the dead
To sing a requiem and such rest to her
As to peace-parted souls.
Laertes.   Lay her i' the earth,
And from her fair and unpolluted flesh
May violets spring! I tell thee, churlish priest,
A minist'ring angel shall my sister be,
When thou liest howling.
Hamlet.   What, the fair Ophelia!
Queen. (scattering flowers) Sweets to the sweet: farewell!
I hop'd thou shouldst have been my Hamlet's wife,
I thought thy bride-bed to have deck'd, sweet maid,
And not have strew'd thy grave.
Laertes.   O, treble woe
Fall ten times double on that cursed head
Whose wicked deed thy most ingenious sense

Depriv'd thee of! Hold off the earth a while,
Till I have caught her once more in mine arms:
Leaps into the grave
Now pile your dust upon the quick and dead,
Till of this flat a mountain you have made
To o'ertop old Pelion, or the skyish head
Of blue Olympus.
Hamlet. (*advancing*) What is he whose grief
  Bears such an emphasis? whose phrase of sorrow
  Conjures the wand'ring stars, and makes them stand
  Like wonder-wounded hearers? This is I,
  Hamlet the Dane.   *Leaps into the grave*
Laertes. The devil take thy soul!   *Grappling with him*
Hamlet.   Thou pray'st not well.
  I prithee take thy fingers from my throat;
  For, though I am not splenitive and rash,
  Yet have I in me something dangerous,
  Which let thy wisdom fear. Hold off thy hand.
King. Pluck them asunder.
Queen.   Hamlet, Hamlet!
All.   Gentlemen,—
Horatio. Good my lord, be quiet.
The Attendants part them, and they
come out of the grave
Hamlet. Why, I will fight with him upon this theme
  Until my eyelids will no longer wag.
Queen. O my son, what theme?
Hamlet. I lov'd Ophelia: forty thousand brothers
  Could not, with all their quantity of love,
  Make up my sum. What wilt thou do for her?
King. O, he is mad, Laertes.
Queen. For love of God, forbear him.
Hamlet. 'Swounds, show me what thou 'lt do:
  Woo 't weep? woo 't fight? [woo 't fast?] woo 't tear
    thyself?
  Woo 't drink up esill? eat a crocodile?
  I'll do 't. Dost come here to whine?

To outface me with leaping in her grave?
Be buried quick with her, and so will I:
And, if thou prate of mountains, let them throw
Millions of acres on us, till our ground,
Singeing his pate against the burning zone,
Make Ossa like a wart! Nay, an thou 'lt mouth,
I'll rant as well as thou.
Queen.   This is mere madness:
And thus a while the fit will work on him;
Anon, as patient as the female dove
When that her golden couplets are disclos'd,
His silence will sit drooping.
Hamlet.   Hear you, sir;
What is the reason that you use me thus?
I lov'd you ever: but it is no matter;
Let Hercules himself do what he may,
The cat will mew, and dog will have his day.   *Exit*
King. I pray thee, good Horatio, wait upon him.

Exit Horatio

(*to Laertes*) Strengthen your patience in our last night's
    speech;
We'll put the matter to the present push.
Good Gertrude, set some watch over your son.
This grave shall have a living monument:
An hour of quiet shortly shall we see;
Till then in patience our proceeding be.   *Exeunt*

Scene II

A hall in the castle

Enter Hamlet and Horatio

Hamlet. So much for this, sir: now shall you see the other;
  You do remember all the circumstance?
Horatio. Remember it, my lord!
Hamlet. Sir, in my heart there was a kind of fighting,
  That would not let me sleep: methought I lay
  Worse than the mutines in the bilbo. Rashly,
  And prais'd be rashness for it, let us know,
  Our indiscretion sometime serves us well
  When our deep plots do pall, and that should learn us
  There's a divinity that shapes our ends,
  Rough-hew them how we will,
Horatio.   That is most certain.
Hamlet. Up from my cabin,
  My sea-gown scarf'd about me, in the dark
  Grop'd I to find out them, had my desire,
  Finger'd their packet, and in fine withdrew
  To mine own room again; making so bold,
  My fears forgetting manners, to unseal
  Their grand commission; where I found, Horatio,
  A royal knavery, an exact command,
  Larded with many several sorts of reasons,
  Importing Denmark's health, and England's too,
  With, ho! such bugs and goblins in my life,
  That, on the supervise, no leisure bated,
  No, not to stay the grinding of the axe,
  My head should be struck off.
Horatio.   Is 't possible?
Hamlet. Here's the commission, read it at more leisure.
  But wilt thou hear now how I did proceed?
Horatio. I beseech you.

Hamlet. Being thus be-netted round with villanies,—
　Or I could make a prologue to my brains,
　They had begun the play,—I sat me down,
　Devis'd a new commission, wrote it fair:
　I once did hold it, as our statists do,
　A baseness to write fair, and labour'd much
　How to forget that learning, but, sir, now
　It did me yeoman's service: wilt thou know
　The effect of what I wrote?
Horatio. 　　　　　　　　Ay, good my lord.
Hamlet. An earnest conjuration from the king,
　As England was his faithful tributary,
　As love between them like the palm might flourish,
　As peace should still her wheaten garland wear
　And stand a comma 'tween their amities,
　And many such-like 'As'es' of great charge,
　That, on the view and knowing of these contents,
　Without debatement further, more or less,
　He should those bearers put to sudden death,
　Not shriving-time allow'd.
Horatio. 　　　　　　　　How was this seal'd?
Hamlet. Why, even in that was heaven ordinant.
　I had my father's signet in my purse,
　Which was the model of that Danish seal:
　Folded the writ up in the form of the other,
　Subscrib'd it, gave 't the impression, plac'd it safely,
　The changeling never known. Now, the next day
　Was our sea-fight; and what to this was sequent
　Thou know'st already.
Horatio. So Guildenstern and Rosencrantz go to 't.
Hamlet. {Why, man, they did make love to this employ-
　　ment;}
　They are not near my conscience; their defeat
　Does by their own insinuation grow:
　'Tis dangerous when the baser nature comes
　Between the pass and fell incensed points
　Of mighty opposites.
Horatio. 　　　　　　　Why, what a king is this!

Hamlet. Does it not, think'st thee, stand me now upon—
He that hath kill'd my king, and whor'd my mother,
Popp'd in between the election and my hopes,
Thrown out his angle for my proper life,
And with such cozenage—is 't not perfect conscience,
{To quit him with this arm? and is 't not to be damn'd,
To let this canker of our nature come
In further evil?

Horatio. It must be shortly known to him from England
What is the issue of the business there.

Hamlet. It will be short: the interim is mine;
And a man's life's no more than to say 'One.'
But I am very sorry, good Horatio,
That to Laertes I forgot myself;
For, by the image of my cause, I see
The portraiture of his: I'll court his favours:
But, sure, the bravery of his grief did put me
Into a towering passion.

Horatio.   Peace! who comes here?}

Enter Osric

Osric. Your lordship is right welcome back to Denmark.

Hamlet. I humbly thank you, sir. (*to Horatio*) Dost know
this water-fly?

Horatio. No, my good lord.

Hamlet. Thy state is the more gracious, for 'tis a vice to
know him. He hath much land, and fertile: let a beast be
lord of beasts, and his crib shall stand at the king's mess:
'tis a chough, but, as I say, spacious in the possession of
dirt.

Osric. Sweet lord, if your lordship were at leisure, I should
impart a thing to you from his majesty.

Hamlet. I will receive it, sir, with all diligence of spirit.
Your bonnet to his right use, 'tis for the head.

Osric. I thank your lordship, it is very hot.

Hamlet. No, believe me, 'tis very cold, the wind is northerly.

Osric. It is indifferent cold, my lord, indeed.

Hamlet. But yet methinks it is very sultry and hot, or my complexion—

Osric. Exceedingly, my lord; it is very sultry, as 'twere I cannot tell how: my lord, his majesty bade me signify to you that he has laid a great wager on your head: sir, this is the matter—

Hamlet. I beseech you, remember—

Hamlet moves him to put on his hat

Osric. Nay, good my lord, for my ease, in good faith. [Sir, here is newly come to court Laertes; believe me, an absolute gentleman, full of most excellent differences, of very soft society, and great showing: indeed, to speak sellingly of him, he is the card or calendar of gentry; for you shall find in him the continent of what parts a gentleman would see.

Hamlet. Sir, his definement suffers no perdition in you, though, I know, to divide him inventorially would dizzy the arithmetic of memory, and yet but yaw neither, in respect of his quick sail. But in the verity of extolment, I take him to be a soul of great article, and his infusion of such dearth and rareness, as, to make true diction of him, his semblable is his mirror, and who else would trace him, his umbrage, nothing more.

Osric. Your lordship speaks most infallibly of him.

Hamlet. The concernancy, sir? why do we wrap the gentleman in our more rawer breath?

Osric. Sir?

Horatio. Is 't not possible to understand in another tongue? You will to 't, sir, really.

Hamlet. What imports the nomination of this gentleman?

Osric. Of Laertes?

Horatio. His purse is empty already; all 's golden words are spent.

Hamlet. Of him, sir.

Osric. I know you are not ignorant—

Hamlet. I would you did, sir; yet, in faith, if you did, it would not much approve me. Well, sir?]

Osric. You are not ignorant of what excellence Laertes is—

[*Hamlet.* I dare not confess that, lest I should compare with

him in excellence; but to know a man well were to know
himself.

Osric. I mean, sir, for his weapon; but in the imputation
laid on him, by them in his meed, he's unfellow'd.]

Hamlet. What's his weapon?

Osric. Rapier and dagger.

Hamlet. That's two of his weapons: but, well.

Osric. The king, sir, hath wager'd with him six Barbary
horses, against the which he has impawn'd, as I take it,
six French rapiers and poniards, with their assigns, as
girdle, hanger, and so: three of the carriages, in faith,
are very dear to fancy, very responsive to the hilts, most
delicate carriages, and of very liberal conceit.

Hamlet. What call you the carriages?

[*Horatio.* I knew you must be edified by the margent ere
you had done.]

Osric. The carriages, sir, are the hangers.

Hamlet. The phrase would be more germane to the matter
if we could carry a cannon by our sides: I would it be
hangers till then. But on: six Barbary horses against six
French swords, their assigns, and three liberal-conceited
carriages; that's the French bet against the Danish. Why
is this all you call it?

Osric. The king, sir, hath laid, sir, that in a dozen passes
between yourself and him, he shall not exceed you three
hits: he hath laid on twelve for nine; and it would come
to immediate trial if your lordship would vouchsafe the
answer.

Hamlet. How if I answer 'no'?

Osric. I mean, my lord, the opposition of your person in
trial.

Hamlet. Sir, I will walk here in the hall: if it please his majesty (it is the breathing time of day with me) let the
foils be brought, the gentleman willing, and the king hold
his purpose, I will win for him an I can: if not, I will gain
nothing but my shame, and the odd hits.

Osric. Shall I deliver you so?

Hamlet. To this effect, sir, after what flourish your nature
will.

Osric. I commend my duty to your lordship.

Hamlet. Yours, {yours.} (*exit Osric*) He does well to commend it himself; there are no tongues else for 's turn.

Horatio. This lapwing runs away with the shell on his head.

Hamlet. 'A did comply with his dug before he sucked it. Thus has he—and many more of the same breed that I know the drossy age dotes on—only got the tune of the time and outward habit of encounter; a kind of yesty collection, which carries them through and through the most fond and winnowed opinions; and do but blow them to their trial, the bubbles are out.

[*Enter a Lord*

Lord. My lord, his majesty commended him to you by young Osric, who brings back to him, that you attend him in the hall: he sends to know if your pleasure hold to play with Laertes, or that you will take longer time?

Hamlet. I am constant to my purposes; they follow the king's pleasure: if his fitness speaks, mine is ready; now or whensoever, provided I be so able as now.

Lord. The king and queen and all are coming down.

Hamlet. In happy time.

Lord. The queen desires you to use some gentle entertainment to Laertes before you fall to play.

Hamlet. She well instructs me.   *Exit Lord*]

Horatio. You will lose, my lord.

Hamlet. I do not think so; since he went into France, I have been in continual practice; I shall win at the odds. Thou wouldst not think how ill all 's here about my heart, but it is no matter.

Horatio. Nay, good my lord,—

Hamlet. It is but foolery; but it is such a kind of gain-giving as would perhaps trouble a woman.

Horatio. If your mind dislike any thing, obey it. I will forestal their repair hither, and say you are not fit.

Hamlet. Not a whit; we defy augury: there is special providence in the fall of a sparrow. If it be now, 'tis not to come; if it be not to come, it will be now; if it be not now, yet it will come: the readiness is all; since no man

of ought he leaves, knows what is 't to leave betimes,
let be.

[*A table prepared; trumpets, drums, and Officers with cushions:
King, Queen, and all the State; foils, daggers, and Laertes*]
{*Enter King, Queen, Laertes, and Lords, Osric and other Attendants with foils and gauntlets; a table and flagons of wine
on it*}

King. Come, Hamlet, come, and take this hand from me.
               The King puts Laertes' hand into Hamlet's
Hamlet. Give me your pardon, sir: I have done you wrong;
  But pardon 't, as you are a gentleman.
  This presence knows,
  And you must needs have heard, how I am punish'd
  With a sore distraction. What I have done,
  That might your nature, honour, and exception
  Roughly awake, I here proclaim was madness.
  Was 't Hamlet wrong'd Laertes? Never Hamlet.
  If Hamlet from himself be ta'en away,
  And when he's not himself does wrong Laertes,
  Then Hamlet does it not, Hamlet denies it.
  Who does it then? His madness. If 't be so,
  Hamlet is of the faction that is wrong'd;
  His madness is poor Hamlet's enemy.
  {Sir, in this audience,}
  Let my disclaiming from a purpos'd evil
  Free me so far in your most generous thoughts,
  That I have shot my arrow o'er the house,
  And hurt my brother.
Laertes.   I am satisfied in nature,
  Whose motive, in this case, should stir me most
  To my revenge: but in my terms of honour
  I stand aloof, and will no reconcilement,
  Till by some elder masters of known honour
  I have a voice and precedent of peace,
  To keep my name ungor'd. But all that time
  I do receive your offer'd love like love
  And will not wrong it.

Hamlet.   I embrace it freely,
  And will this brother's wager frankly play.
  Give us the foils. {Come on.}
Laertes.   Come, one for me.
Hamlet. I'll be your foil, Laertes: in mine ignorance
  Your skill shall, like a star i' the darkest night,
  Stick fiery off indeed.
Laertes.   You mock me, sir.
Hamlet. No, by this hand.
King. Give them the foils, young Osric. Cousin Hamlet,
  You know the wager?
Hamlet.   Very well, my lord;
  Your grace has laid the odds o' the weaker side.
King. I do not fear it; I have seen you both:
  But since he is better, we have therefore odds.
Laertes. This is too heavy; let me see another.
Hamlet. This likes me well. These foils have all a length?
                                      They prepare to play
Osric. Ay, my good lord.
King. Set me the stoups of wine upon that table.
  If Hamlet give the first or second hit,
  Or quit in answer of the third exchange,
  Let all the battlements their ordnance fire;
  The king shall drink to Hamlet's better breath,
  And in the cup an union shall he throw,
  Richer than that which four successive kings
  In Denmark's crown have worn. Give me the cups;
  And let the kettle to the trumpet speak,
  The trumpet to the cannoneer without,
  The cannons to the heavens, the heaven to earth,
  'Now the king drinks to Hamlet.' Come, begin;
  And you, the judges, bear a wary eye.
                                      Trumpets the while
Hamlet. Come on, sir.
Laertes.   Come, my lord.   *They play*
Hamlet.   One.
Laertes.   No.
Hamlet.   Judgement.
Osric. A hit, a very palpable hit.

Drum, trumpets, and shot
Flourish, a piece goes off

Laertes. Well, again.

King. Stay, give me drink. Hamlet, this pearl is thine;
Here's to thy health; give him the cup.

Hamlet. I'll play this bout first, set it by a while.
Come. (*They play.*) Another hit; what say you?

Laertes. {A touch, a touch,} I do confess 't.

King. Our son shall win.

Queen.   He's fat and scant of breath.
Here, Hamlet, take my napkin, rub thy brows:
The queen carouses to thy fortune, Hamlet.

Hamlet. Good madam!

King.   Gertrude, do not drink.

Queen. I will, my lord; I pray you, pardon me.

King. (*aside*) It is the poison'd cup; it is too late.

Hamlet. I dare not drink yet, madam; by and by.

Queen. Come, let me wipe thy face.

Laertes. My lord, I'll hit him now.

King.   I do not think 't.

Laertes. (*aside*) And yet it is almost against my conscience.

Hamlet. Come for the third, Laertes: you do but dally;
I pray you, pass with your best violence;
I am afeard you make a wanton of me.

Laertes. Say you so? come on.   *They play*

Osric. Nothing neither way.

Laertes. Have at you now!

Laertes wounds Hamlet; then, in scuffling, they
change rapiers, and Hamlet wounds Laertes

King.   Part them; they are incens'd,

Hamlet. Nay, come, again.   *The Queen falls*

Osric.   Look to the queen there, ho!

Horatio. They bleed on both sides. How is it, my lord?

Osric. How is 't, Laertes?

Laertes. Why, as a woodcock to mine own springe, Osric;
I am justly kill'd with mine own treachery.

Hamlet. How does the queen?

King.   She swounds to see them bleed.

Queen. No, no, the drink, the drink,—O my dear Hamlet,—

The drink, the drink! I am poison'd.   *Dies*

Hamlet. O villany! Ho! let the door be lock'd:

    Treachery! seek it out.   *Laertes falls*

Laertes. It is here, Hamlet: {Hamlet,} thou art slain;

    No medicine in the world can do thee good,

    In thee there is not half an hour's life;

    The treacherous instrument is in thy hand,

    Unbated and envenom'd: the foul practice

    Hath turn'd itself on me; lo, here I lie,

    Never to rise again: thy mother's poison'd:

    I can no more: the king, the king's to blame.

Hamlet. The point envenom'd too!

    Then, venom, to thy work.   *Stabs the King*

All. Treason! treason!

King. O, yet defend me, friends; I am but hurt.

Hamlet. Here, thou incestuous, {murderous,} damned Dane,

    Drink off this potion: is thy union here?

    Follow my mother.   *King dies*

Laertes.   He is justly serv'd;

    It is a poison temper'd by himself.

    Exchange forgiveness with me, noble Hamlet:

    Mine and my father's death come not upon thee,

    Nor thine on me!   *Dies*

Hamlet. Heaven make thee free of it! I follow thee.

    I am dead, Horatio. Wretched queen, adieu!

    You that look pale, and tremble at this chance,

    That are but mutes or audience to this act,

    Had I but time—as this fell sergeant death

    Is strict in his arrest—O, I could tell you—

    But let it be. Horatio, I am dead;

    Thou livest; report me and my cause aright

    To the unsatisfied.

Horatio.   Never believe it:

    I am more an antique Roman than a Dane,

    Here's yet some liquor left.

Hamlet.   As thou 'rt a man,

    Give me the cup: let go, by heaven I'll have 't.

    O God, Horatio, what a wounded name,

Things standing thus unknown, shall I leave behind me!
If thou didst ever hold me in thy heart,
Absent thee from felicity a while,
And in this harsh world draw thy breath in pain,
To tell my story.   *March afar off*
     What warlike noise is this?
Osric. Young Fortinbras, with conquest come from Poland,
To the ambassadors of England gives
This warlike volley.
Hamlet.   O, I die, Horatio;
The potent poison quite o'er-crows my spirit:
I cannot live to hear the news from England,
But I do prophesy the election lights
On Fortinbras: he has my dying voice;
So tell him, with the occurrents, more and less,
Which have solicited. The rest is silence. {O, o, o, o!}
          Dies
Horatio. Now cracks a noble heart. Good night, sweet
    prince,
And flights of angels sing thee to thy rest!   *March within*
Why does the drum come hither?

     Enter Fortinbras, and the English Ambassadors, with
         drum, colours, and Attendants

Fortinbras. Where is this sight?
Horatio.   What is it you would see?
If aught of woe, or wonder, cease your search.
Fortinbras. This quarry cries on havoc. O proud death,
What feast is toward in thine eternal cell,
That thou so many princes at a shot
So bloodily hast struck?
First Ambass.   The sight is dismal;
And our affairs from England come too late:
The ears are senseless that should give us hearing,
To tell him his commandment is fulfill'd,
That Rosencrantz and Guildenstern are dead:
Where should we have our thanks?
Horatio.   Not from his mouth
Had it the ability of life to thank you:
He never gave commandment for their death.

But since, so jump upon this bloody question,
You from the Polack wars, and you from England,
Are here arriv'd, give order that these bodies
High on a stage be placed to the view,
And let me speak to the yet unknowing world
How these things came about: so shall you hear
Of carnal, bloody and unnatural acts,
Of accidental judgements, casual slaughters,
Of deaths put on by cunning and forc'd cause,
And, in this upshot, purposes mistook
Fall'n on the inventors' heads: all this can I
Truly deliver.
Fortinbras.   Let us haste to hear it,
And call the noblest to the audience.
For me, with sorrow I embrace my fortune:
I have some rights of memory in this kingdom,
Which now to claim my vantage doth invite me.
Horatio. Of that I shall have also cause to speak,
And from his mouth whose voice will draw on more:
But let this same be presently perform'd,
Even while men's minds are wild, lest more mischance
On plots and errors happen.
Fortinbras.   Let four captains
Bear Hamlet like a soldier to the stage,
For he was likely, had he been put on,
To have proved most royal: and, for his passage,
The soldiers' music and the rite of war
Speak loudly for him.
Take up the bodies: such a sight as this
Becomes the field, but here shows much amiss.
Go, bid the soldiers shoot.   *Exeunt*